INSIDE-OUTSIDE

To Be Continued

Richard Herr

iUniverse, Inc.
Bloomington

Inside-Outside
To Be Continued

iUniverse books may be ordered through booksellers or by contacting:

iUniverse
1663 Liberty Drive
Bloomington, IN 47403
www.iuniverse.com
1-800-Authors (1-800-288-4677)

ISBN: 978-1-4502-8778-4 (pbk)
ISBN: 978-1-4502-8780-7 (cloth)
ISBN: 978-1-4502-8779-1 (ebk)

Printed in the United States of America

iUniverse rev. date: 3/8/2011

FOREWORD

History provides context for evaluating society and culture. History is at its best when it is told by the people who experienced it. And it is most entertaining when those who lived through historically significant times have insights and experiences about the people, places and events that the rest of us learn about mainly through popular culture.

Richard Herr's auto-biography took thirty-two years to write starting when he put pen to paper in the largest walled prison in the world in Jackson, MI. Herr's story does not embellish or fantasize. And yet you won't believe how closely real life sometimes resembles what we see in movies and on TV.

The following pages will take you through the life and times of a man who became a Marine in 1959. In the 60's, after returning to the States, Herr found himself driving a taxi selling advertising and eventually selling cars. It wasn't long before he found himself infatuated with the daughter of Paul Amedeo, "Harry" DeRose. In 1964 he married into the LaCosa Nostra Family, as a "white eyes" and lived and worked within one of the most notoriously famous organized families in our country's history. For a year Herr learned the inside business of organized crime. How to make $100K a day at the track, collect a debt from a Major League 30 game winner, and oh by the way, what really happened to the body of Jimmy P. Hoffa.

Then, in 1967 he was sentenced to a 25-40 year prison sentence for murder and would spend the next twelve years deciding whether to claim innocence and risk parole or continue to have his way on the inside. He had to decide whether the drugs, money, and privileges had on the inside were worth spending the rest of his life proudly innocent but incarcerated.

As you read his story consider spending your 21st birthday on a Chinese Junk and sneaking up the Gulf of Phnom Penh from the South China Sea at two o'clock in the morning. Or what it was like being sentenced to 40 years in prison for a murder you didn't commit. How close to real life are the Hollywood portrayals of organized crime in movies like Goodfellas and Casino? What really happens inside one of the world's largest prisons? How to find a kilo of coke on a Florida beach after selling 100 cars a day.

How does a person ultimately transition from organized crime, bar fights, prison, drugs, and two marriages into the man that has been married for over 30 years and has become one of the most respected, hard working, and charitable people in his small mountain town community?

Work hard, play hard. Inside, Outside. The story of a regular middle class, mid-westerner who has experienced lifetimes worth of fortune, and mis-fortune.

Jeremy Vance

CHAPTER 1

A Murder in Michigan

On a warm Michigan summer day in 1965 a young wife and mother of two was brutally murdered. Her nude body was found near a river bank behind her home a day after she was originally reported missing by the local news media.

The small town of Grand Ledge, located in central Michigan, twenty some miles west of the capitol, was shocked and in disbelief, upon hearing of the town's first reported murder in over 30 years. I was subsequently arrested for that murder.

I know that many people have suffered as much, or more, than I have through this period of time. What hurts the most is knowing that there is nothing that I can do in this lifetime to heal those wounds or to make up for the lost years endured by the members of so many families. I'm sure everyone has heard many stories and versions of what actually happened on that fateful day. I'm equally sure that none of the fables can even come close to what did actually happen. So, let's get to it.

Back in the early 1960's while working at a small independent used car dealership I became involved in a car deal which involved the purchase of a new Oldsmobile '98 from a large local dealer. I brought a Mr. Jack Reynolds onto the lot as a prospective customer, but because of the nature of the sale, my owner had to negotiate with the Oldsmobile dealer on the final purchase of the new car. At a certain point during the closing of the sale, I disassociated myself from the deal and let my owner carry the ball. The only time I ever met or saw Jack's wife, Mrs. Betty Reynolds was the day the papers were signed and they took delivery of the car. At that point in time the deal should have been finalized and into the history books. However, due to some sort of oversight or negligence on my employer's part he didn't notice that Mr. Reynolds had signed his name differently on the bank contract, the registration, and the bill of sale. He used the name Jack Reynolds on one form and John Reynolds on others.

Ultimately, the bank caught the discrepancy and refused to honor the contract until all the names were signed identically. My employer delegated this slight task to me, which I accepted, as there did not appear to be anything unusual involved with getting it done. For several weeks I phoned Mr. Reynolds at his home and office and tried to get him to come to my office to re-sign the documents. He always said he would, but never showed up at the appointed time.

I have never left a job unfinished once I've committed myself to doing it. For some reason this has always been a problem for some people to understand. So, even though I subsequently left the used car dealership to go to work for another local car dealer, I felt I had to complete the job given to me; to have the contracts resigned by Jack Reynolds a-k-a John Reynolds. Further encouragement was by way of my former employer's visits to my house requesting that I complete this one last task of his. I was not angry or upset at this request, and would probably need his influences in the auto business later on, so I promised him I would follow through and take care of the problem.

Failing to get Jack in to my office to sign the papers, I worked towards finding out where he lived. He resided in a small town north west of Lansing by the name of Grand Ledge. Not familiar with the Grand Ledge area I stopped at a local gas station to ask directions. Upon my arrival at the Reynolds' home I was greeted and spoke with an elderly lady who said, "Neither Jack nor his wife were home."

On another occasion during my lunch hour, I again went to their house. On this particular visit Mrs. Reynolds was there. She was doing some work outside in a garden area and dressed in a sun suit. After I introduced myself and described the purpose of my visit, she said, "She needed to call her husband and locate the copies of the papers they had signed." She retreated into the house and made a phone call to her husband.

After she had completed her call I asked if I could use the phone to call my former employer. I wanted to let him know where I was and ask if there was anything else that needed to be done. I called the Kalamazoo sales lot first. No luck. Then I tried the Grand River lot. During this period of time Mrs. Reynolds left me standing in the kitchen while she went to her bedroom to change her clothes. When she came back out I was still on the phone trying to reach my former boss. She walked past me to her daughters who were playing on the back porch. She sternly ordered them to go to a neighbor's house to play for awhile. Begrudgingly, they did as they were told. Now in contact with the Larch lot, I was talking to one of the salesmen, who said the boss was not there, but would be back soon.

My back was turned to Mrs. Reynolds and I was not aware of what she was doing. Subconsciously I felt her presence standing directly behind me when I finally hung up the phone. Sensing danger, a form of paranoia I had picked up while in the Marines, I turned quickly and glimpsed something shiny in her hand. Without hesitation I swung around and struck out toward her thoroughly as I had been taught to do in Karate training. I hit her arm, sending her spinning around; without thinking I slammed my right fist into the side of her head. She dropped immediately to the floor with a thud. She didn't appear unconscious, but I knew that she was seriously injured. There was blood dripping from the point of impact where my fist hit her temple. Her eyes were wide open staring directly at me, appearing frightened and yet unseeing. This was a sight of death that I had experienced before while serving in the Marine Corps.

I have always been ashamed of what I did from this point forward. For the first time in my life I panicked. What had I done? What was I going to do? My only thoughts were to get out of there as quickly as I could. But, I couldn't leave her just lying there in the middle of the floor dying. I picked her up and carried her into the bedroom gently laying her on the bed. No sounds emitted from her. She just stared at me, wide-eyed, pleadingly. I noticed that I got some of her blood on my hands from carrying her into the bedroom and so I went into the bathroom to wash it off. My head was spinning and I noticed a strange buzzing noise that had made its presence within my head. I couldn't think clearly. A sense of panic was creeping further into me.

I immediately fled from the house and returned to work. I did manage to calm down during the drive back to the office but I was in a state of shock and disbelief at what had just happened. As I parked and exited the car I managed to slam my finger in the car door busting it wide open. As my finger began to bleed profusely, I reported back to work. The receptionist on duty applied first aid to my finger injury and suggested that I should go to the company doctor for stitches. I took her advice as my finger was beginning to throb and ache. It took me awhile to find the doctor's office, but I eventually did, and he quickly stitched up my wound.

Later that same evening the local news announced that "A Mrs. Betty Reynolds was reported missing." How could that be? I left her on her bed. The next day her body was found several yards behind her house by a river bank. She had been violently and repeatedly stabbed and left there to die.

Needless to say something was wrong. It didn't make any sense, but in a strange sort of way I was relieved because I knew that I had left her on the bed and certainly had not stabbed her.

A few days later a composite sketch appeared on the front page of the local newspaper which surprisingly resembled me. My mind was reeling as I tried to figure out what to do next. I had another appointment with the doctor that stitched up my finger and figured I had better take care of that. While on my way there, my rear view mirror showed that I was being followed by an unmarked police car. While in the doctors office I could see the detectives surrounding the office through the windows. Upon leaving the office I was arrested and taken to the Lansing Police Department. While there I was questioned, fingerprinted and subjected to a police line-up.

I called my wife Pauline and let her know what had happened. She immediately called an attorney. A Mr. Fred Abood. As luck would have it, another attorney by the name of Leo Farhat was with Abood that night. Farhat had represented me on some old traffic tickets, and suggested that since he was familiar with me he should take the case. Abood relented and this decision probably turned into one of the worse decisions we ever made.

But at that point I didn't care who represented me just as long as they got this mess cleared up and me out of jail. So, in what was to be the first of many mistakes, my life was now in Farhat's hands.

One of the fastest and surest ways to find out who your true friends are, is to either get yourself in trouble or convicted of a crime. I can assure you it is a very revealing experience. It seems that people who you would least expect to come to your aide rally around you and the one's you would normally depend upon the most, somehow seem to disappear into the woodwork.

Probably one of the most painful discoveries I made in this area was the complete and total disregard and silence I received from the person I considered to be my dearest and best friend. This is the person I grew up with, partied with, dated with, fought with, and at one point, lived with. This was the man who was to be my daughters' godfather. This is a person who, at the time of the crime, and afterwards was in a position to help since he was working for the Lansing Police Department. Had the situation been reversed I would have done anything within my power to help him. This is a person I truly loved more than a brother and would've given my life for. This is a person, who after over forty-one long years I've never heard another word from. Nothing since the day of my arrest. Truly, one of the most painful and saddest things in this world is a broken friendship.

Eight and a half months in the Eaton County jail proved to be the most terrifying time of my life. I was placed in a one-man cell within the maximum security section located at the far end of the jail complex. I was totally alone. There were no other prisoners around me. There was no radio, television, magazines or newspapers. I was alone on an iron bed, surrounded by cold gray iron bars and cement walls.

The highlight of each week during those long months was a fifteen minute visit. On Friday afternoons I was allowed to visit with my wife Pauline through a heavy glass partition.

Attorney Farhat seldom came to visit. I expressed my dissatisfaction on numerous occasions as to the way he was handling my case. Farhat was not well liked by Pauline and her family and subsequently we hired a second attorney. Joseph Louisell was out of Detroit and the head and chief counsel representing the Mafia Families in the Mid-West. I liked Joe extremely well and from what I could determine during our visits and from his performance in the courtroom he was extremely intelligent and surely a competent attorney. Farhat did not appreciate the introduction of Louisell into the case by Pauline and her parents, and did not hesitate to apply pressure towards me whenever possible to strengthen his position as chief counsel.

Farhat was local and Louisell was over a hundred miles away in Detroit. So, it was easier for Farhat to control whatever I said because of the emotional state I was in. Eventually, Joe removed himself from the case because according to Farhat he had said, "He couldn't do me any good." I later learned from another attorney that Farhat had told Louisell that, "I didn't want him on the case, and preferred Farhat to him." Nothing was further from the truth. But when I was to find out about this it was much too late. I would have already been sentenced and sent to prison and Joe would have subsequently died of a heart attack. Joe was a great man and a brilliant attorney. Had I have known more about the workings of the law at that time and had not been in the emotional state I was experiencing, there would have been no question as to who would have represented me. Both Pauline and I admired Joe very much, and it was his name that was eventually passed on to our son.

I never felt that Farhat intended to properly represent me. It was a shame as I feel if he would have, things would have worked out a lot differently for me. He was always applying undue pressure towards me and thus I never felt a sense of confidence in his abilities. During this period of time in the county jail I kept a daily diary of my thoughts and the things that happened. In it I expressed such thoughts about Farhat frequently.

Unless you've experienced it, there are no words that will describe the mental and psychological anguish of extended solitary confinement. The thoughts of hopelessness and despair mount daily. Without a doubt the only stabilizing factor in those days that helped me to maintain a certain degree of sanity was the support and almost daily letters from Pauline. I would have certainly lost everything if it wasn't for her strengths and beliefs in me and my innocence.

Along with Pauline's support I was able to devise other forms of entertainment which helped maintain a sense of sanity. I began to draw pictures. I cut the bottom out of a chicken pot pie once served at dinner and made a tin foil basket at which I spent many hours shooting baskets on a miniature make-believe basketball court.

For further entertainment, I began to enjoy harassing one of the guards who always gave me a hard time. By stripping off a door jam from the shower stall and acquiring a broom handle and a large screw I was able to tear up a sheet and use the strips for tie strings. Fastening these things together I constructed a long pole with a hook on the end. With this I could reach through the bars, across the cat walk, and open and/or close windows several yards away. That poor old guard was going nuts for a month wondering how I was getting out of my cell to open and close those windows. He believed that to do so, I would have had to unlock my cell door, unlock the outer door to the hallway, unlock the catwalk door and proceed down to my cell area to open the window. He would try to hide around corners to catch me, peer through the door window, and spend long minutes checking on the various locks to no avail. Eventually there came a time when several deputies raided my cell and confiscated all my clever little tools.

I again found subtle ways to entertain myself and stay sane. Farhat was an avid gum chewer, and when he did make one of his rare visits to see me, he would leave me a pack or two of gum. This I would save up and stuff in cell door locks when going to and from my Friday visits. This was fairly easy to do as the guard always walked in front, leading me to the visiting area. A couple of times I was able to manage a grin while watching a serviceman on his knees replacing a lock I had fouled up with my gum.

As recent history bears out, Eaton County was less orthodox when it came to the distribution of justice and enforcing the law. The Sheriff, the Circuit Judge and my prosecutor at the time have all since been ousted because of wrongdoings, that include lies and tampering with evidence. There were several such incidences in my case; I'll get into those things soon. But one incident that I'll relate didn't bear directly on the legal aspects of my case.

Whenever I was taken to the courthouse I was always handcuffed and always had two or three armed guards around me. On this one particular occasion, after having been locked up for over two months I was notified of a court appearance and escorted to the dressing room by the smallest guard on duty. He was not armed and I was not handcuffed. Almost immediately something didn't feel right.

When we reached the ground floor I noticed there wasn't a soul in sight. Even the control room was deserted. To make things even more tempting, the outside door and garage doors were all wide open.

A pretty sight to be sure. Right down to the shine on the tip of the shoe that was protruding slightly past the corner of the opened garage door.

Turning slowly, I grinned back at the guard and said, "You didn't really think I'd go for that, did you?" He just grinned sheepishly back at me, shrugged his shoulders and continued on to the area where I was to get dressed. When we came back out, it was business as usual once again. Deputies were strangely everywhere. The deputy that originally arrested me was now securing my handcuffs prior to going over to the court house and he was shaking like a leaf. He could hardly fasten them and I tried to settle him down by saying, "I'm sorry, I didn't mean to screw up your day, but don't worry, I won't hurt you for it." I think that pissed him off even more.

There was another time approximately two weeks after my arrest when I was taken to the I.D. room within the Sheriff's Department. Inside was my arresting officer, Thomas Keith, their so-called number one detective. He was a tall thin man sporting a crew cut. He was the fellow in charge of my case. As admitted to on the stand during my preliminary hearing, his extensive training in police investigations consisted of a stint in the National Guard and a correspondence course in criminology through the Institute of Applied Science out of Chicago. The same course, coincidently, that I had taken while a member of the Marine Corps. Such impressive credentials wouldn't have even afforded him a walk-on part in a television cop show. But this was Eaton Counties finest. I believe he had as many as four different jobs in as many years after my arrest. Two different local police agencies, a bartender, a short order cook and then on to whatever he is doing now. I guess I should also include a stint as a crime reporter, as immediately upon my arrest he wrote a few articles for a couple of detective magazines about how clever he was to have captured me.

At any rate, two weeks after my arrest Detective Keith took me to the I.D. room and proceeded to take my fingerprints. Twenty-three sets of fingerprints to be exact.

At the time of my arrest I was fingerprinted once at the Lansing Police Department, and once again at the Eaton County Sheriff's Department. They certainly had enough prints to make identification possible.

I was not aware of Keith's objectives during the second print taking, at least not until a few days later. Or so I thought. I was not truly aware of his objectives until several years later.

Prior to my preliminary hearing, I learned that a kitchen knife was found at the Reynolds' home and that it had a partial print on it that had been identified as mine.

This knife, the assumed murder weapon was not found until two days later. Two days after the murder. According to Mr. Reynolds, it was found in the kitchen waste basket, sitting in plain sight on the top of the trash. This awesome discovery was made after a supposedly thorough search of the area by both State and County officials. Mr. Jack Reynolds is the person who found the knife and called Detective Keith. Supposedly, there were no prints on the handle of the knife but there was a small partial print, about the size of a pencil eraser on the upper blade portion of the knife. This was the entire scope of evidence against me. This is what was to convict me.

I denied ever having a knife out there and that those couldn't be my prints on it. Tests were made and supposedly thirteen points were identified on the print which by law is what is required to establish identity. Still I denied that these could be my prints. But, because of this so-called evidence I was bound over for trial.

On several occasions I had requested to take a lie detector test. The first time Farhat suggested that I take one, I agreed to it, but he never brought the subject up again. Subsequently, I approached him on two other occasions to take the test but he always side-stepped the issue stating that such a test couldn't be admitted as evidence in court anyway.

The sitting Circuit Court Judge, Archie McDonald retired and a new circuit judge was voted into office. A Richard Robinson, who according to Farhat, "was a much better judge," and I would be going before him as his first major case.

I was now into my eighth month in the county jail. Farhat began to make more frequent trips to see me as my trial date was approaching quickly. His trips were solely intended to get me to cop out to second degree murder charges. I refused repeatedly to do so. His pressure became more intense. He sent his investigator once to tempt me to plead insanity. He made my father come to see me. And finally two days before the trial, threatened that if I didn't plead to second degree murder he could no longer represent me, and then I would surely be found guilty of first degree murder and spend the rest of my life in prison.

So, we now come to the point of why someone says he did something that he in fact didn't do. I had spent over eight and a half months in almost solitary confinement with virtually no news of the outside world. I later learned, this is a popular method of brainwashing and personality control as evidenced and used by the Chinese during the Korean conflict. It was common place to isolate their prisoners. They found that coercive persuasion didn't work well when the prisoners were housed two to a cell because between interrogations each man could talk to the other and revalidate his own identity.

Of all of the POW's who returned from the Vietnam conflict, not one man was reported to have lost over 35-40 pounds after years of internment. My weight loss in just eight and a half months was 52 pounds.

My parents told me they couldn't afford any more money. That they would have to sell their house as it was.

Farhat said, "My wife would leave me, I could count on that, and that I would never see my children again. That Jackson was like a big country club and I wouldn't mind it there too much. That I would be out in no more than seven years if I plead guilty to a second degree murder charge."

At this time I think I would have agreed or admitted to anything, no matter how hideous just to get out of that jail. So, in fear, ignorance and mental duress, I agreed to plead guilty to second degree murder. Right or wrong it seemed like the only option I had if I ever expected to see my family and be a free man again.

So, a date was set to take my plea. Pauline would have none of it. She figured it was insane to plead guilty to something I did not do. So she immediately retained an attorney out of Westland, Michigan by the name of Evan Callanan.

On two separate occasions Evan said he tried to see me at the county jail prior to the plea hearing. But the Sheriff on orders from Leo Farhat wouldn't let him in to see me. So, on the day of the court appearance he met me outside the courtroom with Pauline.

We were given about a half an hour together, during which Evan brought up many points of law and discussed pieces of evidence and investigation reports that I had never been made aware of by Farhat.

Such as, why was there a broken window at the house? Why was there blood found in the basement? The very suspicious nature of the finding of the knife two days later. Why were so many prints taken from me? What was the motive? Good questions. What was the motive? I had only met Mrs. Reynolds on one prior occasion and that was only for about five minutes when her and Jack came to the dealership to sign the final loan papers. There was nothing taken or removed from their house. There was no rape or sexual overtones present nor any financial gain to be obtained from such an act. There was only one person that I'm aware of that profited from this murder.

As recorded in the Lansing State Journal the Eaton County Sheriff, Elwin Smith made a statement when asked about a motive, "We don't know that yet. I guess we'll just have to use our imaginations." With police professionals like that handling my case, I didn't stand a chance.

Unfortunately, Evan looked like a bum. His shoes weren't shined. His fingernails were dirty and he just didn't have the look of a successful attorney. I had come too far now and after a half hour Farhat burst into the room like a Syrian bull waving his arms and shouting, "the deal is set. It's your only way out. Don't throw it all away now, think of my reputation." Well, just to show you the state of mind I was in and the control that Farhat had over me, I was actually concerned about "his" reputation.

Unfortunately, the law is a lawyer's game. I have come to believe that lawyers are not interested in the truth. They are interested in money and reputation. Truth is not the point of a trial, just as justice is not the point.

Thus, I thanked Evan for his trouble and went in to plead guilty to second degree murder. As stated in the transcript, I said, "Yes, I did it," to the judge, "but that I didn't know why I did it, when I did it, how I did it or where I did it."

Judge Richard Robinson accepted my plea. At that point I think the reality and enormity of what I just did hit me. I wanted to change my mind. I had Pauline get Callanan back. I fired Farhat on the spot in the courtroom and took Evan on as my attorney. He immediately asked the judge to set aside his acceptance of my plea. Robinson, now clearly upset over this turn of events ordered that Callanan bring his request to him in writing by way of a motion. Callanan did, and was subsequently denied.

I was sentenced two weeks later in March of 1967 to serve a 25-40 year sentence. So much for Farhat's seven years.

I let them beat me. I let them control my mind and break me down. Something I shall always regret. Besides taking these years out of my life for something I didn't do, they cheated me out of the most important moments in life; the birth of my son and daughter and the infancy and growth of my children.

On November 29, 1966, while locked up in the county jail, the birth of my twins, a son and daughter took place. It was while in the county jail, through the thick glass partition that I first laid eyes on my twins, so small and fragile. At least there was one compassionate guard on duty, who allowed me to leave the visiting room to come around to the gate where I could at least reach through the bars and touch my new son and daughter.

At the time I sincerely thought that I was making the right decision. But, it was a decision based solely on the terrified thoughts in my stagnant brain. Without the benefit of counsel or a qualified third party or family member I was trapped and picked what I believed to be the only alternative to a seemingly hopeless situation. I don't know if I can ever forgive myself or them for this hell.

On March 31, 1967 I was taken to the Jackson State Prison in Jackson, Michigan. The facility covered 56.2 acres of space; it was the largest walled prison in the world. The iron doors, and iron gates surrounded iron lives. There is nothing human here. Cold gray walls, cold gray hopes and metal trays for metal food would dictate my life for the next twelve years.

I don't remember all of my first impressions of this place as those iron gates slammed shut behind me. But, I do know it was a frightening experience.

I once wrote a few words for an English assignment while attending Wayne State University that I feel best describes what it was like sitting alone in a prison cell. It went something like this:

In the cell, cold and barren and cluttered, a cracked, scratched frameless mirror reflects stripped and peeling paint. A single dimming 40-watt bulb highlights scarred and paint-stained porcelain as night descends over the cages of human bondage. A cardboard toilet seat barely hides the odors of backed-up excretion, and on the walls between aging Playboy centerfolds, hang the squashed remains of cockroaches that didn't scurry fast enough into the shadows. In the corner, a small radio pulls in the life of another world almost forgotten and growing more unfamiliar and oblivious. Distilled sounds of a hundred senseless activities echo throughout the cavernous iron and fortified enclosure. A single figure sits lifeless on sagging springs, slowly turning the pages of a battered book he doesn't see. Thoughts of time, and why, and bitterness flow unchecked through a mind full of acrid despondency, and depression and self-imposed debasement.

A few days after my arrival at Jackson prison there heralded an explosion in the prison armory that took the lives of two guards. The explosion was so intense that it shook the trays on our tables as I ate one of my first gourmet meals in prison. It seems that a couple of guards were practicing their quick draws and when one of the pistols went off, the bullet struck some other explosives in the room and subsequently destroyed everyone and everything in the immediate area.

After completing twenty-three days of psychological testing I was admitted into the general population of Jackson Prison. During this time I was certain that I would be released soon, as Mr. Callanan was appealing my case and certain that because of the numerous mistakes found in my case it was cut and dried and my sentence would be reversed with no problem. A month passed, then two, then five, and finally a year.

What was going on? Callanan dropped out of sight. He wouldn't answer my letters, nor would he return Pauline's phone calls. So, I had Pauline call the Appeals Court to find out how my appeal was coming along.

What appeal? There was no appeal on record. Callanan had never filed one. Enraged, I filed a grievance with the Michigan Bar Association. At a hearing in Detroit, Callanan was found guilty of negligence and received a formal reprimand. But, nothing was determined as to why he did what he did or did not do. We did not get any of the money that we paid him back. The only thing of interest that I found was that Callanan was a friend of Leo Farhat and that they had attended law school together. Was this some kind of a conspiracy? I don't know for sure, but it certainly smelled of one.

Let me elaborate on that. For many, many years Leo Farhat ran the Prosecutors Office in Ingham County and was very good at his job. Because of his political friends, ambitions and past convictions he was recognized as one of the top prosecuting attorneys in the area if not the state. Thus, when he originally took over my case I naturally figured I could probably do no better. But there was one black spot on Mr. Farhats resume of which I was unaware of at the time. He had spent years in the Prosecutors Office, trying to convict and shut down the business and dealings of my father-in-law, Harry DeRose. This was the primary thorn in his side. Harry was the one that always got away. All that I can figure is, this case could be his way of getting back at the family and achieving some satisfaction to that end. And yes, if you knew Leo Farhat and his Syrian temper, his ego, and quest for fame it's not a hard stretch to believe.

So where did that leave me? No attorney, no money and no appeal. But I had a very courageous wife, one who would not give up. I talked to her about an attorney I had read about out of Houston, Texas by the name of Percy Foreman. I read that he had never lost a case. My case might be something he would be interested in. Mr. Foreman did in fact reply and did express his interest but said that because of how heavy his case load was he wouldn't be able to handle my case for at least another two years. He did say that there was a very up and coming attorney out of Boston, Massachusetts that I might try; A man by the name of F. Lee Bailey. Pauline and I talked about him for sometime and decided to try and take that step. I wrote him several letters and when he made a trip to Detroit, Pauline made a trip there to meet him. He said he was interested. We sent him all of the information we had along with all of the money we had left; a little over ten thousand dollars. An interview was set up, and one day as I was out in the prison yard waiting for him his Lear jet flew over the prison. With a wave of his wings I waited in anticipation for his arrival. I waited, and waited and waited. Well, he finally did show up, but not without a taste of the good old Herr luck first.

It seems that after Pauline picked them up at the airport to drive them to the prison, she had a flat tire. As luck would have it, the spare was also flat. So, here was the world famous F. Lee Bailey and three of his investigators stranded on the highway with no way to move. They eventually reached a local farmhouse where they called a wrecker and sat in the wounded car on the back of a hook, being towed to a local gas station. I'm sure that would have been a humorous sight to see and not an experience Bailey cares to remember.

The Bailey name struck fear in Eaton County for a couple of weeks while his investigators sifted through the evidence and transcripts, (what little there was), and said, "They'd get back with me."

Again, as luck would have it, Bailey became involved in troubles of his own. He was disbarred and kicked out of the state of New Jersey. He was involved in movies, writing books and two much more celebrated cases than mine. I would have to wait. I waited for a year and a half until he again came to Michigan with another famous attorney, Melvin Belli. Pauline again met with them for lunch and returned to me excited about what he was going to do. Then Bailey was off to Florida, Mexico, California and New York; chasing the big bucks.

My case was soon delegated out to a subordinate in the office since it did not merit the publicity that Bailey was used to receiving in his other more celebrated cases. The stall was on; they would get to me soon. Soon developed into years and my impatience and disappointment increased. Then there came the request for more money. No way was I going to throw more money his way, especially when I didn't feel he had done a damn thing for me so far other than make promises and make me wait. We had already given him all the money we had which was a total of ten thousand dollars. I sent Bailey a letter requesting the return of my papers and fired him.

After researching the F. Lee Bailey history I find I would have probably been better off to wait for Mr. Percy Foreman.

Yes, Mr. Bailey got Dr. Sam Shepard out of prison – a whole ten days before his parole took affect. He defended "The Boston Strangler" and got him life in prison as opposed to the death penalty which was eventually received at the hands of another inmate. Then there was New Jersey's Dr. Carl Coppolino that he effectively got a life sentence for. Then there was the "Pied Piper of Tucson" also a life sentence. Thus, upon reflection I guess it was a good thing that he did not defend me. I might still be in prison.

The next attorney on the scene was Theodore Albert. Ted used to work out of Joe Louisell's office at one time and I liked him. I still do, for that matter. He did more for me than any other attorney to date and managed to fit the pieces of the puzzle together, finally.

We found out that the Reynolds children returned home early that day and saw a blue 1962 Ford in the driveway. Thinking someone else was at the house, they returned to their friend's house.

We found out contrary to Mr. Reynold's statement at the time of the crime and hearing, when he had said, "he did not receive a call from his wife and that he did not go home," that he in fact did receive such a call and did in fact go home that afternoon.

A client, who was in Jack's office and accompanied by a friend said when he received the call from his wife he stated, "I have to go home immediately" and rescheduled their appointment for later that day. He borrowed his secretary's car, a 1962 blue Ford and went home. When he returned to work he was wearing different clothes and visibly shaken according to both of his secretaries and his returned client and her friend. Much to the astonishment of Alberts people, neither this client nor his secretaries were ever questioned by the authorities or investigators. On two different occasions at a local bar in Lansing, customers and waitresses reported that Jack had threatened to kill his wife. Their marriage was on the rocks and Jack was the only person with a motive who stood to gain financially and emotionally by his wife's death. On one occasion when leaving the courtroom Jack approached Mr. Louisell. When Joe expressed his sympathies Jack made the statement, "Oh, I don't know, it's like a bad cold. You get over these things." This was a statement made only a few weeks after his wife's death. Strangely enough that Christmas Jack sent Pauline and I Christmas cards stating that if there was anything he could do to help, to not hesitate to ask. Investigators revealed that Mrs. Reynolds had frequently dated other men and had posed for pornographic photos. In fact, Jack stated to several of his friends that someone was doing time for a crime that he committed. The most important evidence was the fingerprint found on the knife which strangely enough was no longer there. A latent print, one placed there physically by someone will remain indefinitely. But, a print that is placed on something after being lifted from somewhere else will eventually dissolve. All of a sudden the reason for Detective Keith taking so many prints from me began to make sense.

Albert got me back in to court in an effort to obtain a reversal. We put Farhat on the stand and in an unprecedented move Farhat began to revealed several pieces of privileged; client/attorney information which was placed into the record. It also came out that in order to gain the confidence of my parents and in-laws, Farhat had shown them a confession that I had supposedly written and signed. Obviously, he could produce no such confession to the court or to us, because no such confession ever existed. But Farhat used this ploy to gain the support of my family and friends to help transfer their loyalties to him and justify the mishandling of my case.

While back in court again, a reporter from the *Lansing State Journal;* Mr. Charlie Haas, was able to see the inconsistencies of the case and was shown some of the new evidence. Charlie wrote two good articles on my behalf before pressure was applied to him from both Farhat's office and his editor. He was subsequently restricted from writing articles on my case.

Later, he was to pay a visit to the prison and we were able to talk alone for a few minutes. He said he would be interested in writing a book about my case if I was willing. I said I was. Shortly thereafter he was fired from the *State Journal* and a few weeks later he was found dead in his home. A man in his early thirties in relatively good shape, I was told that Charlie had somewhat of a drinking problem and supposedly one night he drank just a little too much and when he passed out, he didn't wake up again. Needless to say my suspicions about that death and the circumstances surrounding it are very much alive considering the time and way it supposedly happened.

But Ted had won a small victory in court for me by getting certain information into the record even though Judge Robinson and his dancing kangaroos denied all of his motions.

One incident that took place during these proceedings involved Mafia Tipster Peter Lazarus. While Farhat was on the stand being questioned by Albert, the doors of the courtroom burst open, and Lazarus walked up to the front of the bench like he owned the place. With total disregard to the proceedings that were in progress he began a conversation with Judge Robinson. Neither Albert nor I could believe our eyes or ears that this type of conduct could be allowed. But it was certainly typical of this court's respect for the law and courtroom procedures.

After a few minutes Lazarus turned around and left the room without so much as an apology or acknowledgement for the interruption. Robinson told Albert he could resume his questioning. This is the same judge that several months later sentenced John Sinclair to the same sentence that I received; 25 to 40 years in prison for possession of a marijuana cigarette. Now, there's some equality in sentencing, huh? This is also the same John Sinclair that John Lennon wrote a song about. He and his wife Yoko Ono protested outside the prison on the day that F. Lee Bailey came to see me. These were the late '60's and the days of revolution and the Detroit riots.

CHAPTER 2

In the Beginning

The Herr family has never been what you would call an intimate family. We've never really known that much about each other. I never knew my parents that well and I don't believe my mother and father ever knew their parents very well.

Back in the early 1960's my uncle, Melvin Albert Herr traced the Herr family back to its origins in Germany, to one Christian Herr. Christian Herr was a Mennonite minister who, because of his "radical" beliefs in God was forced to leave Germany. With certain members of his family, he sailed to America in the early years of our country. Upon arriving in America he found that he was still persecuted for his religious beliefs. So, he moved from state to state until he finally settled in what is now called Lancaster, Pennsylvania. This is a town where the majority of Mennonites still reside today and the Mennonite religion still flourishes. In fact, the original home that Christian Herr built there is still standing today as an historical site.

Certain members of the Herr tree remained in Germany. When exactly our branch of the Herr family immigrated to the United States, I do not know. But, I do know that my great grandfather, a soldier in the Kaiser's Army had fought against the United States in World War I.

My father was born in Cleveland, Ohio on September 6, 1917

to Mr. Melvin A. and Mrs. Marion Herr. They named him Richard George Herr. From what I understand, it was a stormy marriage that ultimately ended in divorce. Grandma packed up her two sons; Richard and Melvin and eventually moved to Michigan, where she remarried. She was to be divorced and remarried at least two more times in her life. It was her last husband Earl Blair that I remember most.

Somewhere in those years in an effort to provide for and support herself and two sons, which until recently was a closely guarded secret in the family, Marion found work as a nightclub entertainer and part-time prostitute.

Grandfather Melvin, who once owned a nightclub in the city of Cleveland, was to die in the late 1950's in Cleveland, broke and lonely.

My mother's background is even more sketchy and without detail. Of French origin, she was born in Des Moines, Iowa on August 24, 1918 as Eudora Florence Brucklmayer. Her father was both a fireman and telephone repairman. It was on a stormy night in Iowa, while he was working on a downed power-line that he was accidentally electrocuted and died. Her mother was to remarry and move to Florida. Later in a fit of jealous rage, this man shot and killed her mother and then turned the gun on himself and committed suicide.

Still a young girl, my mother was sent to live with various relatives who shuffled her back and forth from family to family. She was eventually sent to an orphanage where she was ultimately raised by an order of Catholic nuns.

I don't know what type of lives my parents lived as children, as they never felt free to talk to me about it. But I suspect that with the tragedies of death, murder, divorce and their frequent moving, it was a difficult and unsettling life.

They eventually came to meet each other at a dance held at the "In" place of the times in Haslett, Michigan. A place called the "Dells" which, I understand still stands on the banks of Lake Lansing, but is now under new management and a new name.

I was born, raised, and grew up in Lansing, Michigan. I was born on the 13th day in May, 1941 at St. Lawrence Hospital at 8:30 p.m. I was named after my father, Richard George Herr. At the time of my birth, my father was in the army and stationed at Camp Blanding, right outside of Jacksonville, Florida. It was here that my mother took me to live for a couple of years until my father was discharged from the army. He was a Master Sergeant and instructor for those men who were to leave for Europe and fight for the United States in World War II. Unfortunately, most of those men he trained would later die at the infamous; "Battle of the Bulge".

Following the war and dad's discharge, we all returned to Lansing, Michigan. My father went to work for Sears Roebuck and Company. With the exception of a small stint as the person inside the giant Planters Peanut costume, who would walk up and down the streets of Lansing hawking peanuts, he spent his entire working life at Sears. Starting out as a stock boy, he worked his way up to a Divisional Manager. He was to give 33 years of his life to Sears Roebuck and Company before retiring and moving to Fort Myers, Florida with mother in 1972.

I really don't remember that much of my early childhood. I don't remember it to be a particularly unhappy or distressing one. But, then it is said, "You only remember the happy times of your life," and if that's so, maybe that explains a lot of the gaps in it.

The first home I remember living in was a two-family house on Massachusetts Street in Northeast Lansing. It was a short distance from someone we called Grandma O'Brien. To this day, I'm still not sure what type of relative grandma O'Brien was to our family. But, I think her son; Obie O'Brien was grandma Herr's second or third husband. I used to enjoy going over to their house to see Obie. Obie would play games with me and give me handfuls of peanuts to eat. He seemed to have a passion for peanuts and would also give me the money to go buy them. This is also the house we lived in when my sister, Carol was born on September 27, 1945.

From there we moved to 834 Cawood Street on Lansing's Northwest side. Here is where my childhood seemed to flourish. I attended Verlinden Street School from kindergarten to the fifth grade. It was while living on Cawood Street that my second sister, Judy was born on October 23, 1947. There was not much of a relationship between myself and my sisters, at this time, because I'm sure I felt so much older than them. Shoot! They hadn't even started school yet, and Judy couldn't event talk. What fun were they?

I do have flashes of those early days and some of the firsts that took place in my life. It was in kindergarten during recess, after a hard morning of building blocks that I received my first kiss from a girl. I can still remember her name. Somehow I got roped into playing house and, of course I got assigned the roll of daddy. It was just a gentle kiss on the cheek, but I never forgot it. The only other incident I can remember with a girl back then was when I was wrongly accused of shoving a young female classmate in front of a car on Saginaw Street. Evidently her new dress was torn and she had to come up with an excuse fast. Since I was one of the kids who walked with her to school each day, I was the lucky one to get the blame. Her father came over to our house in a rage, and despite my cries of innocence, I was properly beaten by my father with his belt. It wasn't until the next day that the girl's father again came over to the house to apologize for his daughter, who finally admitted to lying about the incident. But, I never forgot that punishment. When I was later to attend high school with both of these young ladies, they had both developed into very beautiful girls, indeed. The girl with the torn dress became our Homecoming Queen and the other was a princess in her court.

While living on Cawood Street the big past-time was playing cowboys and Indians, which I played with a passion. There was no television back then and when dusk approached we gathered around the radio to listen to such favorites as; "Sky King", the "Lone Ranger", the "Green Hornet", the "Fat Man" and many other exciting plays and serials on the radio.

At one time, I was appointed the leader of the gang on our block. Not because I was any kind of a macho strong or a clever kid, but because my parents had the only garage on the block that you could lock the doors on. In there, my loyal comrades and I could all hide out from the more vicious gang members on Comfort Street. As an example, my gang consisted of five members; one totally blind kid, a deaf-mute, another who wore braces on both of his legs, and a normal kid who was to become my best friend. Along with myself, of course, also considered normal at that time. In contrast, the leader of the Comfort Street gang grew up to be strongman, Mr. Michigan. I should have known then the direction my life was taking. But, we did share many good experiences together and believe it or not, we actually won a few of the skirmishes we were involved in.

Our favorite form of battle was rock throwing, for which it seems I was forever getting in trouble because of the number of broken windows I was credited with at the end of each day.

My best friend's father was on the Lansing Police Force and famous among all the kids in the city at the time as he used to visit all the schools and perform magic tricks with a wooden dummy called "Safety Sam", in the promotion of safety among the kids.

Christmas time, as were all Christmas' when our family was together, were the happiest times of my life. It seemed that all the family came together then with the Aunts, Uncles, Grandparents and friends. Even dad and mom were different people then. Once I remember dad filled our backyard with hundreds of Christmas trees which he sold from there. The food, the gifts, the laughter and the excitement of Christmas mornings are times I shall always cherish.

But, when Christmas wasn't around; it seems that dad and mom were always too busy doing their things. I can't speak for my sisters, but I think I always felt like an outsider. When other kids' fathers were playing with them at the ball games in the empty field at the end of the block or building race carts, or any other number of things, my dad was always too busy. So, I went to my best friend's dad for entertainment. I went to another friend's father for help on my race cart. It was my uncle Mel who eventually taught me how to fish and play tennis. Mel was a stage actor and comedian and a good one at that. He was very well known by everyone in Lansing. He was president of the Lansing Civic Players and for a while the General Manager of the Lansing Civic Center. That was really neat because he always got me into all the concerts and shows that were staged there. I was able to go back stage and on a couple of occasions I met people like James Brown. And I had four visits with Johnny Cash. They were two entertainers I really admired. It was the time of MoTown, so I saw and met them all. Little Richard, the Supremes, Marvin Gaye, the Temptations, Jackie Wilson, and on and on. Stevie Wonder who was at the time attending the Michigan School for the Blind in Lansing was just appearing on the scene. I'll never forget his first appearance on the stage of the Lansing Civic Center after his introduction. You could see a hand behind the curtain pushing him out to do his song. The poor kid just kept walking to the sound of the audience with no clue as to where he was going. Suddenly there came a hush over the audience as we watched him moving towards the orchestra pit. Fortunately an alert handler back stage could see what was about to happen and quickly ran out to grab him before he feel into the pit. Obviously his career has been incident free of that type of management since.

I was around the age of ten or eleven when we packed up and moved again. This time to 1209 Lenore Avenue on Lansing's Southwest side, near Colonial Village. We were moving up in the world now, to better and newer houses and neighborhoods.

Here I began school at Elmhurst, and even though I met many new friends, I never left my old ones. Often on weekends we would peddle our bikes across town to see each other. At Elmhurst I began to play football and cops and robbers mixed in with the cowboys and Indians. Though these games were beginning to fade out now to baseball and football, in the streets.

Shortly after moving to the house on Lenore Avenue my uncle Mel got me a part in a television commercial. We made three-one-minute ads for Reo Lawn Mowers. The filming took place at a large mansion on the north side of Lansing. This was the Dodge Mansion built by the Dodge brothers of Dodge Automobile Manufacturing fame. Mel played the part of my father, who in one sequence was sleeping peacefully in a hammock as I excitedly ran up to him to inform him of the arrival of our new lawn mower. Another ad demonstrated how easy the self driven mowers were to operate, since even I, a kid, could handle it with ease. So could grandma. Or at least a young lady dressed up to look elderly. She was seen running or dragged off into the sunset by the self powered mower.

The filming itself took one or two days to complete, but was fun and rewarding when paid with a $50.00 savings bond and a legal excuse to be away from school. Not to mention the chance to see see yourself daily on television.

I was never a big kid and didn't start to really put meat and muscle on my bones until after I joined the Marine Corps. So, it was easy for me to get pushed around. It seemed to happen frequently enough until one day when the local bully shoved by sister Carol on the ground. Well now, you can shove me, or I can shove my sister, but you or no one else can shove my sister. So, completely forgetting that I was terrified of this bully and his equally tough brothers, I attacked. We must have fought for three blocks. Through yards and bushes and flower beds, tearing up lawns and shrubbery; ending in exhaustion somewhere near his house where we both finally decided a truce was in order. I don't believe either one of us won the fight, but we were both bruised, crying and our clothes were a tattered mess. But the result was he never shoved my sister again and we ultimately became good friends. My respect around the school and neighborhood elevated considerably

After completing the sixth grade at Elmhurst, I transferred to Walter French Junior High. Here, after a few semesters of failing grades my parents took me out and enrolled me at St. Casimirs, a Catholic school, much smaller and strictly run by a group of "Our Sisters of Mercy" nuns.

It was at St. Casimirs that I learned a lot about life, both physically and mentally. All of a sudden girls seemed more important than electric trains. I was in junior high school and that was a new status in life. Education became important and tiresome. But, it was here that I learned the most and received my best grades. The nuns would allow no fooling around and ruled with an iron hand and battle scared yardsticks. Classes were strictly regimented and each day started with early mass, a must to attend.

It was while at St. Casimirs that I started my first real job. I became a paper boy for the Detroit Free Press. Now, the Detroit Free Press is a morning newspaper, and since I was still required to be at mass the first thing each morning you can imagine how early I had to get up each day. Plus, I took over the route of 101 customers in the middle of winter. But, for better than a year I managed to get up every morning to fold and roll papers, and then off on my bike in the icy cold to deliver papers to customers scattered all over the south side of Lansing and still show up for early mass. Then between homework hours it was out at night to collect. But it was a profitable job, and I managed to save up enough money for what I really wanted; a new J.C. Higgins bike. A real beauty with two baskets mounted on the rear, streamers on the handlebars, a horn, a radio, two rearview mirrors, white sidewall tires and a big head light. A real treasure in those days that peddled like a John Deere tractor pulling a wagon load of logs. But it sure helped to build up the muscles in my legs which turned out to be a blessing in later years once I joined the Marine Corps.

The other two money making jobs I had at this time while going to St. Casimirs, was mowing lawns in the summer and shoveling walks and driveways in the winter. I managed to establish a regular group of customers at this time and was able to make extra spending money to buy the things I needed. Dad always complained that everyone else's lawns were mowed, and their walks and driveways shoveled, but ours never was. He was right. But then, it was just a matter of economics. The other's paid cash. He didn't.

It was also at St. Casimirs that I learned to do other things that I'm not so proud of. In an effort to be "one of the guys", I fell in with the wrong group. There were about ten kids who consisted of the "in" group, and to be accepted, you had to do certain things. The group consisted of both boys and girls and we would go into the area drug stores on Barnes and Logan Streets, and while one member of the group distracted the druggist, the others would fill their pockets with candy, gum and comic books. This eventually became a weekly occurrence.

Then on Sundays, while everyone was at mass, a few of us would sneak out to meet in the parking lot. There we would find a car with the keys still in the ignition and go joy riding. This was an era when people trusted one another and leaving the keys in your car while you went to church or ran into a store for a short while was common place. Try doing that in today's world and you'll be shopping for a new car or dealing with an insurance company. But, we would somehow always make it back before mass ended. Luckily, we were never caught. Although, maybe if we would have been apprehended our outlook on life would have been a little different.

There came a time while at St. Casimirs that upon reaching the pinnacle of a ninth grade freshman, the Sister, (Nun) assigned the class a project. Every year in Lansing and the surrounding area they have what is called a "Youth Talent Contest." Our class project was that everyone would enter something in this contest. My particular assignment was a total of 26 pictures that I had to draw. Now, this particular nun was a strange breed. She was the terror of the school who did not believe in spare the rod and spoil the child. Daily she would wield her pointer or yardstick on someone. Often she would discipline someone over her chair at the front of the classroom, usually a girl, and then make the rest of the class put their heads on their hands while she lifted the unfortunate girl's dress above her waist and proceeded to apply the appropriate whacks with the ruler. Needless to say, in those days that would be the highlight of the day for us boys. We peeked. But, in her twisted sense of justice if a boy screwed up she would take us to the faculty kitchen down the hallway, where we would be made to drop our pants to receive our punishment with a yardstick. A humiliating situation to be sure. Wonder how that would go over in today's world?

Well, there was just no way that I would be able to finish 26 pictures in the time allotted. So, when school let out at 3:00 p.m., I was held after to complete my assignment. As the clock was about to strike 6:00 p.m., I had still only completed four pictures. In a fury, this vision of black and white terror came at me with her yardstick. After receiving a few whacks on the knuckles, I decided enough was enough and tore the yardstick out of her hands and broke it into many small pieces and threw them at her. Then in my rage, I chased her all the way back to the safety of her convent.

I went home scared to death and told my parents what had happened. The next day my mother and I were standing before the Mother Superior explaining my behavior. I was not expelled, but was switched to a different class and different teacher.

The high point of that event was that when the Youth Talent competition ended, I was the only member of the class that won anything. I received an Honorable Mention ribbon for the four drawings that I did finish and enter, a plaque, my name in the newspaper and a smile of satisfaction on my face.

St. Casimirs only went through the ninth grade, so I was given the option of continuing on in a parochial school, meaning St. Mary's, or transferring back to a public school, J.W. Sexton. Because of the tuition and slight financial difficulties at the time, I opted for Sexton.

What a change Sexton was from St. Casimirs. To me it was a regular blackboard jungle .The largest high school in the area at that time with well over 3,500 students.

Because of the better education I received at St. Casimirs, my sophomore year at Sexton was fairly easy for me and I breezed through that year without applying myself to much.

Discipline at Sexton, at that time, was almost nonexistent. Almost daily there was a fist fight in the classrooms or corridors between teachers and students, and students versus student, male and female alike.

Sexton is an old school and dates back a long way. Before being called Sexton it was called Central High School, and both my father and his brother, my uncle Mel, attended and graduated from there. In my years at Sexton I even had a couple of the same teachers my father had. A Mr. Devereux, who taught biology and Mr. Harold Lantz of the history department.

I'm sure you've all seen the popular television program "Happy Days". I think my parents saw me as the Ritchie Cunningham type and always dressed me that way, much to my displeasure. I saw myself as the Fonzie type and that's the way I tried to live when away from home. At school I was considered a hood and hung around with these types, because they were the "in" group and the dominant force throughout the school. Nobody messed with us or they had to answer to the rest of the gang. I did still participate in such conforming activities as tennis, football and the chess club. I've always liked those sports and still do today. But it was here at Sexton that I first started to skip classes and then entire days of school. A group of us, both boys and girls, would go to various houses whose parents were away or at work and we would sit around listening to records, dancing, drinking beer and necking.

One thing a group of us would do each day is to extort money from the other kids. We would patrol the school hallways and in a very intimidating manner ask for pennies, nickels and dimes from the other kids, both boys and girls alike.

Even though I'm sure we became a daily nuisance, no one ever reported us or questioned our motives. Usually by lunch time we had accumulated enough money to join the other kids at the local restaurant for hamburgers and malts.

I got into a lot of fights then and believe I won a good majority of them, although I did lose a few. Many such fights were with our cross-town rivals at Eastern High School. Sexton and Eastern high schools were the only two large public high schools at the time in the city. There was always a very strong rivalry between the two, and if we weren't invading each others' territory during the day, we would challenge each other at the local dances. The largest and most popular was the National Teen Club (NTC) dance held each weekend at the Civic Center.

There were always parties afterward called grassers, where we would all chip in for a keg of beer and find an empty field somewhere and get roaring drunk before being raided by the police. Luckily, I was never caught in one of those raids, but did have a few close calls.

It was during this time that I began to work out and train for the

Golden Gloves in Lansing. Dad had always liked boxing, so I thought if I became a fighter I could get his attention now and then. It did seem to impress him at the time and for a short while I trained pretty hard. Al Van Ness, who was my coach at the time, and later became somewhat of a legend in the Golden Gloves in Lansing was always impressed with my jab. He said it; ..."was as powerful and more effective than most fighter's punches."

We trained in the Caravan, a building situated on the corner of Saginaw and Grand Avenue. Since I lived on the other-side of town, in Colonial Village, it soon became somewhat of a chore walking, running, or hitchhiking the ten or twelve round trip miles every evening, especially in the winter time. Hell, I wore myself out just getting there to work out. So, after about four or five months the lure of gaining fame in the boxing ring wore off and I decided to call it quits before I even got into any tournaments. Although, I did have several exhibition fights in the gym, which I did well in. I am sure Al was disappointed when I quit as he thought I could have been a pretty good fighter. But the distance I had to travel each evening just became too exhausting. Especially the return trips home in the late evening and after a strenuous workout. I did enjoy the times I spent there and learned a lot about self defense. I probably would have continued in the sport if I had lived a little closer or had a means of transportation to or from the gym. I'm sure a truly dedicated pugilist would be ashamed of my reason for dropping out, but I guess at that time, at sixteen years old, I just wasn't that dedicated.

The first girl I ever went steady with was both popular and beautiful. We began to date and went to various school functions together and it was from her that I first learned the soft touch and tenderness of the opposite sex. We dated for several months before I lost her to a football hero and the biggest kid in school. I don't remember his name but he was huge. He was approximately six foot six and weighed in at around 250 pounds. At any rate, my pride was hurt so for a couple of days each time I passed him in the hallway I would bump into him on purpose trying to provoke him into a fight. Well, I finally got my wish. Figuring that I would probably continue to taunt him until he confronted me he accepted the challenge. Actually, it didn't turn out to be much of a fight. I don't think I landed even one blow the entire time. Being so big he had the advantage of reach also and commenced to bounce blow after blow off my forehead raising welts and bruises all over my face. To make matters worse, he somehow got his thumb hooked in my pants pocket and practically tore my trousers off of me leaving me to stand in the middle of the school hallway in my underwear. Fortunately there was a restroom nearby and I quickly retreated to the safety of that enclosure to suffer my embarrassment in semi-privacy. I never taunted him again.

The next important relationship with a girl in my life was with a Michigan State University Sophomore. Although, at this particular time, I was still a junior in high school.

One of the favorite past-times of kids in Lansing at the time, was to cruise the "strip", which consisted of driving back and forth up and down Washington Avenue from Main to Saginaw Street. Every night thousands of cars and kids met here after dark to pick up girls and guys, challenging each other to fights and drag races.

It was on one of these nights, while cruising the strip, that I met my college fantasy. She was driving her new Plymouth Fury convertible with her girl friends. Somehow I must have said something clever and talked her into pulling over and a new relationship began. It was somewhat of a status symbol to be going with her at that time. After all she was older and a college student. She was also from a moderately wealthy family. Her father was a vice-president of Reo Motors and they lived in one of the nicest suburbs in Ingham County, Forest Hills.

We went together for over a year. I often snuck out of my bedroom window and met her a block away from our street in her car after I was supposedly in bed. From there we would attend various parties and necking sessions. I got away with this little trick for quite awhile before my mother found out and locked all the doors and windows on me. Needless to say that was an exciting night when I got home.

But being the love struck fool that I was; I was soon meeting the love of my life again at night. This time I helped her crawl through my bedroom window and when mom would check on me, she would hide in the closet. I don't believe my mother ever knew that secret part of my romantic life.

During that time we would visit her grandmother on Kalamazoo Avenue and it is here that a Pauline DeRose used to watch me without my seeing or acknowledging her existence

Pauline used to live next door to my then girl friends grandmother, and also my uncle Mel and another good friend of mine that I ran with. All of these folks lived on the same block so she had often seen me around yet we had never formally met.

Of course, there came a time when my college romance and I parted ways. But, before we did we experienced the less of our virginity together. It was a very tender, special, exciting and beautiful moment.

It was also while I was going with this lovely lady that I had my first brush with the law. On one particular night she came to my window and wanted me to go somewhere with her but due to the risk involved I decided I'd better not chance it. She became angry and left. After she left I became worried about our relationship together, so still in my bright orange pajamas, I decided to do a crazy thing. I climbed out of my bedroom window and rolled my father's car down the driveway and part of the way down the block. I figured I could catch her and straighten this thing out. So, around two o'clock in the morning I was speeding through East Lansing, when I caught sight of a police car circling around the boulevard to catch me. Knowing I didn't have my license with me, or permission to use the car, I attempted to lose him in the winding streets of East Lansing. I did quite well, turning corners on two wheels, sliding up and down streets, until I no longer could see him behind me. But to be on the safe side I pulled up into the driveway of a large red brick house and parked. I slid down on the front seat. After about ten minutes when I thought the coast was clear I rose up and attempted to start the car. You can imagine my surprise when the police car that was chasing me pulled up behind me. Not being familiar with the city of East Lansing, it just so happens that of all the driveways I had to pick from, I chose the one belonging to the East Lansing Police Department which was an old converted house. Such luck, I can't believe.

While still in my bright orange day-glow pajamas I was escorted inside and given a ticket for speeding, eluding an officer, and can you believe, indecent exposure, even though I was completely covered. But pajamas are not considered to be proper street attire, so. . .

My father, of course, was awakened and told to come to pick me up. He was not smiling when he got there. I was ultimately restricted to the house for the next several weeks and when he took me to appear in court I received a suspended sentence and had to pay the court costs. Our breakup was short lived and eventually the young lady and

I did get back together but it became a little harder to see her after that experience.

The majority of my teen years were fun and exciting and I was always on the go. My sisters were a pain in the neck and we had our battles from time to time but as each year passed I felt we grew closer and closer together.

I was in my teens when I got my first summer job as a busboy at the Senate Grill, a popular eating establishment in those days. I eventually ended up doing a wide range of jobs there, from washing dishes, to peeling potatoes to short order cook. I enjoyed the job and made a few dollars. Then for three summers I would caddy at the Lansing Country Club. Although it was tiring and exhausting work, I enjoyed it immensely and made good money. Half of which, much to my chagrin, I always had to hand over to my mother who would save it for me to purchase school clothes and supplies with.

When mother started to do that I started to put half in my shoe before I got home. That way she only got half of a half. I figured, if I earned it, I should have a say in where it went.

One of the best times of the year for our family was dad's vacation. We would take two to three weeks every summer and rent a cottage at Scenic Lodge in North Muskegon on Lake Michigan. The beaches were beautiful and the water crystal clear. Probably my most pleasurable moments and memories rest in this part of the world. I still often return there to see it and rest and think. There's not much left of the place anymore, due to the erosion, but the memories still linger. It was here that I first learned how to play tennis, water ski, ride a horse, swim and fell deeply in love.

It was to a girl three or four years my junior. She was without a doubt, the most beautiful, tender, and precious and caring person I had ever met. I went with her for over three years and don't know if I ever loved a girl as much as I did her.

During this relationship my parents again moved. This time to the small village of Okemos and the status symbol of River Downs, right next to the prestigious community of Forest Hills. It was a beautiful sprawling ranch house with lots of yard. I loved it as much as I'm sure the entire family did.

But to complete this move I had to drop out of Sexton in the middle of my senior year. When told I would have to start the twelfth grade over again at Okemos High School because they didn't have half year classes, I opted to call it quits for school.

At the time I didn't realize how important graduating and proms were. I would give anything to change and relive that part of my life again. One of the problems that my new love and I experienced in our relationship was that I lived in Okemos, Michigan and she lived in Joliet, Illinois. Needless to say this was a considerable distance to commute. But through constant letters, our summers together and numerous hitch-hiking trips to her home on weekends and holidays, we were able to continue our relationship.

Now came a point in time when I had to decide between continuing my education, getting a job or going into the service. I had always had a special place in my heart for the United States Marine Corps and knew that sooner or later I would pursue that avocation. Unfortunately, due to certain circumstances my decision to join the Marine Corps came sooner than later.

One hot muggy summer evening in Michigan I received a phone call from my good best friend. "Hey Richard, I met a couple of girls that want to party tonight. Are you ready?" Hum! Let's see. Two horney guys in their late teens with two young horney teen girls who want to party. Seemed like an awful dumb question to me. So, a half hour later, my friend was at my front door to pick me up in his father's company car.

Did I mention earlier that my friend's father was a lieutenant in the Lansing Police Department? Back then, certain police personnel were allowed to take their assigned vehicles home with them. At this particular time of the year his parents were on a two week family vacation, minus my friend, who elected to stay home. Thus, the only vehicle that he had access to was in his garage. A fully contained, marked and lighted Lansing Police cruiser.

Well, ok this should be interesting. "Are you sure this is ok?" I asked. "Get in, we're wasting time." So off we went to the other side of town to meet our dates. Of course, when we drove up into their driveway they were a little nervous seeing us arrive in a police car. But after a couple of minutes assuring them we really weren't the law, the party was on.

Eventually the conversation turned to drinking and how the girls had done their share at various parties, and that they never got drunk, and that alcohol never affected them. My friend looked at me; I looked at him; sounds like a challenge to us. So off we went to Comfort Woods to dig up a few bottles of booze out of a stash we had buried there a few months earlier, also using dad's police car, but that's another story.

After we got back to the girls' house, we went inside, and one of the girls pulled four large drinking glasses from a cupboard and handed each of us a glass. We had figured that two fifths of Jack Daniels should do the trick. My wide eyed friend then pours the first girl a half a glass of straight Jack, to which she replies, "Fill it up." My friend shrugs his shoulders and complies with her request. The second girl also requests a full glass. She got it. Then, as my friend pours each of us a shot into our glasses, the girls both chug theirs to empty. Both my buddy and I look unbelievably at each other, as they offer both their glasses back for a refill. My friend complies, and the same results follow. Both girls down both glasses with seemingly no effect. My friend and I still have not taken a drink. Once again, the girls hold out their glasses for another refill. We look at each other. "Could this be real?" My happy friend starts to oblige them and gets half way through the third refill when one of the girls throws her half glass on the other and starts laughing uncontrollably. The now wet, head to toe, girl looks down at herself and starts to strip naked. My friend looks at me again and putting his arm around the dressed lass starts walking her off to the bedroom with a smile and a wink. As they pass out of sight into another room I look at my designated young lady and grin; she looks at me, turns, and runs out the back door of the house screaming at the top of her lungs. I stand there, stunned, my ego shattered. I can't believe I looked that bad. I ran after my shirtless friend to a back bedroom who already has his young lady semi stripped down and tell him what happened. "Well, go get her for Christ's sake." he says. "Ok, that sounds sensible." So, off I go, out the front door and down the street looking for my lost love. To the end of the street and around the block I frantically run. No naked young girl to be found. So, back to the house I return to my semi-happy and now frustrated friend. "What now?" I ask. "Okay", he shouts. "Everyone into the car," and off we go searching for our naked nymph. Up one street, and then down another, searching the neighborhood thoroughly. Finally, over the police radio comes a disturbance call occurring on Indiana Avenue of a naked white female who was banging on doors and causing a commotion before passings out on a front lawn. We were just turning on Indiana Avenue and sure enough, a crowd was forming in front of a house around a naked figure lying on a front yard. Sirens from approaching police and emergency vehicles could be heard in the distance. A few people out front saw us approaching in the police car and started waving at us and pointing at the body on the ground. I can just imagine what was going through their minds as we quickly sped up, turned the next corner and got the hell out of there, and headed back to the girls house. After all, it just wouldn't be right if we would have stopped there, two teenage boys in a police car, with a half naked teenage girl sitting between us. We dropped the girl off at her house; my friend dropped me off, and he headed for home, undetected. He locked his dad's police car back up in his garage.

The next day passes. Nothing. Another day passes. Nothing. I call my friend, "What's going on?" "I don't know." He replies. "Are your parents still on vacation?" I ask. "Yup" he answers. A week passes and nothing. Did we luck out? The girls didn't necessarily know who we were. I sure as hell didn't know either of their names. Very quickly, over a week and a half passes and still nothing. Now, it's our family off for a well deserved three week vacation on the beaches of Lake Michigan. The first week was a bit apprehensive waiting for God knows what. But, I still received no call or information. Was it possible there was no problem?

Too soon our vacation was over and we were back to Lansing. Dad's off to work. Mom's putting lunch remnants away and the door bell rings. A quick look out the window reveals a very familiar looking Lansing police car at the curb. Mom opens the door and standing tall in full uniform was my friends' dad. He was a very, very upset and mad friend's dad. As he enters the house his hat goes flying across the room, "of all the God Damn stupid idiotic things to do." He shouts at mom, who has no clue of what he's talking about.

It seems that after the ambulance picked up our passed out naked nymph, and took her to the hospital, she stayed passed out for several weeks. Her partner for one reason or another wasn't talking about it and it wasn't until she came out of her coma, approximately four weeks later, that her parents along with the Lansing Police Department put the pieces of the puzzle together. We were soon directed by my friends' father to turn ourselves in and report to a couple of detectives and make a statement. I'm not sure how, but apparently the detectives were able to exert enough pressure on the girls parents to prevent them from filing charges. They then strongly persuaded my friend and I that we should keep a very low profile for a while. A suggestion was also made that military service might be a way to achieve such a low profile. I always wanted to join the Marines, so I did. My friend, who was still working his way through high school, finally graduated and followed me into the Marines.

CHAPTER 3

The Best of the Best

On September 22, 1959 I became a Marine. I enlisted for four years, which at that time was the shortest enlistment period one could volunteer for. Besides, the Marines were the best and I loved the uniform. Boot camp in the Marines at that time was probably the hardest test of physical and mental endurance that I or any young man at that time had ever been subjected to. For the next three months all I did was run. There were only two ways to get anywhere in Boot Camp and that was to run or march and if you were caught not doing those options your life would be unbearable. Yes, I've seen unbearable. It's called STP or STU, (Special Training Platoon or Special Training Unit) and I didn't want to go there. For recreation on the weekends our platoon would be split up on the football field facing each other and then at the sound of a drill instructors whistle we would rush each other and which ever team was able to pull, push, or drag the other team across the goal line would win. Anything goes short of using a weapon. Sounds like fun, huh? Well, call me warped, but it was fun. For a little diversity they would throw a huge ball between us and getting the ball across the opponents' goal line would count as a point. Again, anything goes. Once during bayonet training we used what was called a "pugil-stick" to simulate a bayonet and rifle butt. Both ends of the stick were wrapped so when you attacked your opponent you didn't hurt him too bad. On one occasion I was doing pretty good and knocking off the enemy one after another when the next guy up was a rather emaciated young guy wearing double thick glasses and very vulnerable. But, being a good recruit I attacked him quick and sending his glasses flying in one direction and giving him a vertical butt stroke between the legs he went down hard grabbing at his crotch and rolling around on the ground in shear agony. So figuring I won, I stopped. "What the hell do you think you're doing?" shouted the DI. "That Jap is still alive. He could be fooling you. Kill him." "But sir," I pleaded knowing this poor kid is really hurting. "Kill him" the DI screamed at me. So winding up, I slammed the end of my stick into the side of the poor guys head. "That should do it," the DI said, as I turned to face my next attacker. But, being a bit unraveled from the last attack, the next guy up, who was much smaller than I, deftly fell to his knees and got through my defenses and nailed me in the gut with the bayonet end of his stick and now I was out. "Well, what in the hell are you waiting for recruit." The DI yelled at me, "Get over there and find recruit xxxxx's glasses, apologize to him and help him up." The marches, the hikes and overall training were unrelenting and at times unbearable. But, I don't regret a minute of it. Once you finally got through Boot Camp and earned the title of a Marine, there was nothing you couldn't do or live through from that moment on. Upon graduation from boot camp I was ordered to a headquarters company and attached to an 81-mm mortar section at Camp Margarita, the home of the Fifth Marines, inside Camp Pendleton.

When I first joined the Marine Corps I was sent packing to San Diego, California for basic training. The love of my life back in Joliet and I became engaged to be married. I was happier than I'd ever been in my life. But unknown to me at this time, my parents were against the match. It was only recently that I found out that my mother had sabotaged the engagement when she wrote a letter to my fiancé outlining some of my shortcomings, the least of which was my not being a high school graduate.

Shortly thereafter, at Camp Pendleton, I received a "Dear John" letter and the engagement ring from my love. It was the most crushing blow of my life and there was nothing I could do from that distance to salvage the romance, though I tried.

I spent almost two years stationed in California. I traveled the state extensively from San Diego to San Francisco and Oakland. I met many new friends, shared many new experiences and saw many movie stars' homes. I attended a few opening nights, at the movies, and even met some of the stars. I met up with Leslie Gore a noted singer and recording artist of the time after a concert in San Diego and was able to take her and her girl friend to lunch. One of my friends in the platoon went to school with Annette Funicello, and he took me to see her on break from one of her movies in Hollywood and she served us apple pie and milk in her apartment. I water-skied under the Golden Gate Bridge, and got stuck on a sand bar in San Francisco Bay on a friends speedboat. I went across the border into Tijuana, Mexico, watched the bull fights and Jai Alai games and other sorted sports in the red light district. I bought my first car; a 1950 Ford Coup convertible, black with a white top. I completed a G.E.D. test and got my high school equivalency certificate. I visited Disneyland, the New Pike at Long Beach and dated a telephone operator from Oxnard.

Once during a mock war problem called, "Operation Green Light," at Camp Pendleton, I was being flown into the rendezvous area from the deck of an aircraft carrier by a helicopter that had me strapped beneath it in a Mighty Mite, a small compact version of a jeep. It just so happened this particular squadron of helicopters was being flown by reservists. As we came upon the drop-zone, evidently the pilot took the phrase, "drop-zone" literally, and from about forty feet off the ground, he released the hook that was holding me a bit early. So, down I dropped, sitting in the seat of my trusty Mighty-Mite, when I hit the ground on the side of a hill. We hit hard, we bounced hard and I flew out of the jeep over the back end and landed hard. Somehow I still managed to hold onto my rifle, but when I looked up; I saw that the worse wasn't over with yet. Here came my jeep rolling towards me, fast. That small jeep hit me and underneath it I went with my rifle tangled up in my arms and legs. The one thing that I remember most as I managed to open one eye is the sight of the front axel hitting me square in the nose and knocking me back down. I swear all four wheels must have rolled over me. Luckily, if anything can be considered luck at this point, most of the batteries that I was carrying in the Mighty-Mite had also bounced out when we first hit so the weight of the jeep wasn't all that bad. Otherwise it surely would have crushed me far worse than it did. Once the jeep had continued it's journey down the hill, I laid flat on the ground in shock and semi-consciousness, when a couple of guys ran up to me to see if I was alive or not. Somehow I managed to get to my feet. But I had trouble seeing, as my poor nose was smashed almost flat so I couldn't see past it. I raised one arm, and then as I attempted to raise the other, I passed out and crumpled to the ground. Later, when I regained consciousness, I was laying in a field hospital, along side what appeared to be several other Marines and with a red tag tied to my big toe that read, "Killed in action." Needless to say that is not the most comforting sight one would like to see upon regaining consciousness.

Once it was established that I wasn't a deceased casualty I was loaded into a military ambulance; and that became one of the most painful trips I've ever taken. I was driven back to the base hospital, where I was put in casts, taped and bandaged up enough to qualify for a part in a new mummy movie. Thus, for the next couple of months I got to lie around the barracks convalescing and eating through a straw. This unfortunately was also the time I received my Dear John letter. Not a happy few weeks to say the least.

The entire "Green Light" operation was to eventually be the worst the Marine Corps was ever to have staged. The chopper that was to come in right after mine ran into some high tension wires, and five men were killed in that one. Presumably these were the bodies that I had seen lying next to me when I regained consciousness. Later, supposedly because of a wrong fuel mixture, several trucks and an Antose blew up, killing their occupants. An Antose is a tank like vehicle with six large 105 cannons mounted on it verses the one cannon you see on a tank.

I earned my Private First Class (PFC) and Lance Corporal Stripes and became a squad leader. I became an expert with the M-1 rifle and a sharpshooter with the 45 caliber pistol. Then, it was time for us to board ship, and we were off on our much anticipated trip to the small island of Okinawa where we would be based for the next thirteen months.

Our first stop was at Yokohama, Japan where we were introduced to the delights and strangeness of a new country. I found Japan to be a marvelous and fascinating country, unlike anyplace I'd ever seen. Unfortunately we just spent a day in Yokohama before we were off again to the island of Okinawa. Upon arriving in Okinawa, we were housed first at an Army base named, Sukiran, outside the village of Fatima, and then on to the newly opening Camp Hansen on the other side of the island near the small village of Kin.

Okinawa was another great experience, and outside of the on-going Marine training, I met many new friends among the villagers. One such friend was Mariko Tomashiro, a young seventeen-year old Okinawan girl. We hit it off together right away. It was my first night in town and her first night as a hostess in the Grand Hotel. She was scared to death and her girl-friends were trying to guard her closely. But, we hit it off right away and eventually were to become constant companions for the next three months. I took her to her first American movie, taught her how to roller skate and play cards. She taught me about the black-market and how to hide from the military police. Then, our battalion was ordered to setup base in Japan for the next couple of months. Mariko was crushed and didn't want me to leave. She never thought I would come back to her. On our last night together, she cried, begged and pleaded for me not to leave. She offered to hide me, work for me, anything, so long as I didn't leave. I swear, that's the closest I ever came to going AWOL. Never had I had anyone throw themselves so completely at me. It was tough to leave her, but I had to and did. When I did return to Okinawa several months later, I searched hard for her, from city to city. But, she disappeared and I never saw her again.

While still in Okinawa I happened to pass through a small village by the name of Kin .There I saw an exhibition in Karate demonstrated by Enzio Shimabutu. He was the only true holder of a red-belt at that time, and a true master in the art of Karate. He was in the process of opening a new dojo (school) and was looking for new students. The incredible feats he performed were so unbelievable and impressive that I had to learn more about this skill. So, I became the only American in a class of about twelve students, and for the next two years, I practiced the art of Karate hard and faithfully every day, seven days a week.

From Okinawa we would begin to make periodic excursions to other countries. We went back to Japan and camped at the base of Mt. Fuji, without a doubt the most beautiful mountain in the world, except maybe when you're climbing it which I did on three occasions. When you're in the Marine Corps, and there's a mountain nearby, which there always seems to be, you'll eventually end up climbing it.

While in Japan I visited Yokosuka on numerous occasions. I shopped on the Ginza and ate dinner in the world's largest night club. I visited the Tokyo Tower and had Christmas dinner at the home of the American Ambassador to Japan, Edwin Reischauer and his family.

This was 1961 and the USO had managed to set this little affair up with various other servicemen during the Christmas season with other American families who lived in and around Japan at the time. I just happened to draw Mr. Reischauer and it turned out to be a wonderful dinner and evening well spent.

From Japan we went to Korea. We set up camp near some little village on the coast very near the 38th parallel to prepare us for our cold weather training. Korea is without a doubt the most miserable country for a foreigner on this earth, at least in the middle of January it is. It smelled awful, probably due to the human escheatment they used to fertilize their fields. The people were incredibly poor and I've never known such cold. Anyone who fought there in the war deserves a medal just for surviving it. But, the people were nice and after spending a festive night with a Korean family, I do carry some positive feelings of the place.

On one particular night, there were three of us who left our pup-tent camp, and ventured into the outskirts of the village. There we were invited into the house of a family where we were asked to share some homemade wine/sake with them, and between drinking that, and smoking from a community pipe that contained a type of opium, the three of us became quite senseless. We spent several hours there singing and sharing customs. Sometime during these festivities we all passed out and when we regained consciousness, we were at the edge of the creek, across from which our camp was setup. That little Korean family had somehow managed to carry all three of us heavy Marines, in our heavy cold weather gear along with our untouched weapons the three miles back to the base. A feat in itself to be sure which also displayed the honesty and integrity of a poor people.

But the hardest part was yet to come. We had to get across that creek and back to our tents. Somehow, the other two Marines managed to jump across the stepping stones to the other side. Me, I got about halfway before I fell through the ice and sat in the middle of the creek splashing away and having a great time before the other two pulled me out. We eventually made it back to our respective tents where I passed out again on my sleeping bag only to wake up the next morning a solid sheet of ice. Everything was frozen stiff and I thought for sure I was going to die. I've never been so cold in my life. But somehow I managed to break out of my clothes and shake the ice off while I stood around in my birthday suit drinking coffee by a fire in a 55 gallon drum. It was also in Korea that I got lost in some snow covered mountains while on patrol. As a forward observer my radio operator and I were attached to a line company while they played war games. Sometime during the evening hours we both fell asleep and were subsequently covered in snow. When we awoke we immediately noticed that the platoon we were attached to had moved out during the night and had forgotten something; us. My radio operator then gleefully informed me that we had a dead radio and communication was non-existent. We would now have to find our way back to civilization with a hope that we didn't accidently cross the 38th parallel and into the arms of the North Korean Army. A few anxious moments there to be sure, but fortunately I was well trained in how to read topographical maps and was able to locate a mountain road that I felt sure would take us back to our creek and camp. I'm happy to report that it did, as an approaching search and rescue jeep stopped and picked us up.

We also hit three different islands in the Philippines. It was here that I met a very proud and fun loving people. They wear their hearts on their sleeves and show an outward affection for Americans. I loved the Philippines and it is my ideal vision of paradise. A life's dream is to go back there to live out my life. But one I sadly won't fulfill, I'm sure. I had several nice and interesting experiences while there.

While in Subic Bay we lived aboard ship. All our dress uniforms and civilian clothes were stored in the bottom of sea bags, so they were usually in no shape to wear. Once, when returning from five days in the field we were allowed to go to the servicemen's club on the base, as we were, in our boots and utilities. It was a beautiful, newly built place and one of the nicest enlisted men's clubs I'd seen. So, in strolled a little less than fifty of us dirty, unshaven, fatigue wearing Marines, to do some serious drinking. There were probably a hundred sailors in the club already, dressed in their pretty whites. A small Philippine band was playing on the stage and all was going along well for about an hour. Then, as it seems will invariably happen whenever a bunch of sailors and Marines get together, the peace was soon shattered. It seems that one party of Marines had grown tired of the music the band was playing and decided to turn the jukebox on. The Navy fellows didn't like that idea, so they unplugged the jukebox. The Marines plugged it back in. The sailors unplugged it. The Marine plugged it back in. The sailor started to unplug it again, and as he was bent over, the Marine slammed his chair over the sailor's back and then all hell broke loose. One of my more weird aspirations in life was to get into a good bar brawl, and this was it. The entire nightclub erupted. There were bottles, chairs, fists and bodies flying everywhere. The band fled the stage just as a chair went through the drums. Two walls of picture windows were shattered by bottles and chairs. That brand new naval enlisted club was soon turned into a shambles. It looked like World War III had just broken out.

I, of course got in my licks, punching out a few of the Navy's finest before someone hollered out that the Shore Patrol was coming. All of us tore out of there as fast as we could and headed back to the ship where we were met by the Officer of the Day, who began handing out MP arm bands. He told us to go to the enlisted men's club where there was a report of a large fight in progress. So, shrugging our shoulders, why not, we put on the arm bands and headed back to the club to help quell the disturbance. I think we arrested every sailor we found, but strangely enough, couldn't even find one Marine to arrest. We chuckled about that little experience for weeks afterward.

While on another island, in the Philippines, I met a cute little gal, who went by the name of "Peanut". She was full of energy and love. She made me feel like the king of the island. We made love on the beaches, swam in small inland bays, showered under waterfalls, paddled in outrigger canoes and picnicked in the jungle. It was a glimpse of paradise that I pray I'll never forget.

While still on another island outside the village of San Jose I met an old doctor who shared his house with me and enjoyed telling me stories about the atrocities of the Japanese occupation. He introduced me to the chief of a tribe of Mon Yons who took me to their grass hut village where I shared in an open pit feast put on by the villagers. These are a people and country I shall always remember and cherish forever. The Mon Yons are a tribe of people that should be featured in "National Geographic" magazine and probably have been. They wear a loin cloth; carry a spear and very crude and intimidating machetes. From time to time, according to the doctor, they war with another tribe of Mon Yons, on the other side of the mountain, who are head hunters and cannibals. They supposedly wear tails attached to their loin cloths that are not permitted to ever touch the ground. When they sleep they supposedly insert the tail in a hollowed out coconut.

The only reason I had the privilege of meeting them was because they came out of the mountains to watch the landings of the huge C-130's touching down and unloading their cargos of tanks, trucks, jeeps and Marines. They were totally awe-struck at how these things could fly and land with so much inside of them. It was really quite fun watching the incredulous expressions on their faces. Ever seen the old Abbott and Costello movies where they give the chief a lighter in the darkest recesses of the Amazon Jungle, and the chief goes gaga over it? Same reaction when I gave the chief of this tribe a Bic lighter. This was a totally incredible experience for him to see fire coming from a blue plastic stick.

One evening while sitting with a few friends in a local nightclub, I happened to look across the room to see one of the most elegant and beautiful ladies I have had the pleasure to see in the past eight plus months. She was a striking dish-water blonde who looked totally out of place in these particular surroundings. She was presently being mobbed by a bunch of sailors, who I'm sure, besides being appraised as the prettiest thing around, was also the first white woman any of us had seen in many months. After awhile the mob seemed to thin out around her, and being a bit lit myself by this time, I thought, what the hell, I'd try my luck. Well, it seems the fates were with me because she readily welcomed my company and in a few minutes requested that we leave that particular nightclub for another. So, giving my fellow companions the big wink, I was off on a very enjoyable evening. We hit another local bar and then had dinner together before continuing our tour of the local nightclub scene. Barbara B., it seems, was a small time French actress. She was presently in the Philippines filming a black and white movie called, "Valley of the Dragons," a low budget movie that you can occasionally pickup on late night television. At any rate, we had a lot of fun together and I played the roll to the hilt especially anytime we crossed paths with other servicemen, seeing as how I was the only one in town with a 'round-eye', and a truly gorgeous one at that. But, my bubble burst when later in her hotel room after enjoying her company, I found out it wasn't necessarily my magnificent body she was after, after all. Knowing that our ship was scheduled to dock in Hong Kong within the next two weeks, she wanted me to meet her there where she would give me a package containing a certain amount of heroin. I was then supposed to smuggle that package back to the United States and be paid accordingly. "Being a serviceman and in particular an NCO, you will have nothing to worry about," she said. Well, I'm afraid that such games of intrigue at that time just did not excite me, and much to her displeasure I declined her tempting offer. What the hell, I got what I was after, and possibly helped in teaching her a few facts about the world of business in the meantime. But the way she looked, and what she was offering and promised I'm sure she eventually got the job done.

During a particular night out on the town in Olongapo, we were all suddenly rousted out of our favorite bars by the military police and ordered back to our ships. Returning to my ship, the USS Navarro, I was told to pack up my gear and move to the aircraft carrier, Valley Forge. Several months earlier I was promoted to corporal and named a section leader in charge of twenty-two men.

Now, if I might regress for a moment, the promotion to corporal and an NCO is somewhat of an interesting tale. Our commanding officer at that time, whose name unfortunately escapes me, was one you could conclude was of the old corps. Meaning that he was tough, no nonsense and very serious about the training of his men. But, if you did your job, and did it right, there were rewards. One of his little passions was a five mile run every morning before breakfast, seven days a week, no exceptions. Many a day, many of us would start a run half dead with a hangover from the night before. At the end of five miles, we were all now sober and hungry. Still the best cure for a hangover, I know of.

One of the captain's rewards was, if we performed our duties well, we would be treated to a "smoker". A smoker consisted of finding a deserted beach somewhere, where the beer, steaks and all the fixings' were provided, along with a boxing ring, where we could work off all our aggressions. On this particular occasion he had an added treat for us. The heavy weight boxing champion of the US Army was there to put on an exhibition. He first fought a couple of rounds with a couple of his Army buddies and then asked for volunteers out of the audience. A couple of inebriated Marines volunteered and were quickly dispatched in the first round. Well, we couldn't have some dog face come into our party and show us up. So, with half a keg of Budweiser in me for courage I stepped into the ring at the protest of my captain. "Lance

Corporal Herr, get out of there, you've had too much to drink. "No" I can take him, Captain", I said, once again disobeying his order to get out of the ring. "Alright, let him get himself killed," the CO responded, with a clear look of displeasure on his face.

Clang! The first round begins and Sgt. Jones commences to rain down blow after blow upon my body but failing to knock me down or out. We went on to the second round which was pretty much the same as the first, except he was slowly knocking me sober. Round three and I was pissed. So, reaching back to the days of the Golden Gloves and more recent Karate training I exploded out of my corner determined to teach this showoff not to mess with the Marines. I brushed away all of Jones' defenses and drove him back and forth across the ring. Finally, I hit him hard enough to put him down. But, instead of retreating to a neutral corner I followed him down and straddling his chest continued to pummel his head and chest until I was pulled forcefully from him and removed from the ring to the cheers of my squad and platoon.

The next morning, after our five mile run, we were in formation in front of the CO's office. Instead of being dismissed for breakfast we were directed to stay in formation. Out came the captain, and positioning himself in front of us called out, "Lance Corporal Herr, front and center." Oh, shit! I've had it now. With a gulp, I left the formation and stood at attention in front of the captain. The platoon was called to attention and the captain proceeded to give an orientation on what a Marine was. What we're made of and what's expected of us. Yesterday Corporal Herr stood up to that call, and showed the Army we don't quit. By now my head was buzzing. What's he saying? I'm not going to the brig? What? "Congratulations Corporal Herr", the captain said, as he handed me my Corporal stripes. "Dismissed."

Back to the story and being transferred to the aircraft carrier, the Valley Forge. It wasn't until two days later, on May 13, 1962, on my twenty-first birthday, that we were all told to report to various holds in the ship to draw live ammunition. I was issued live rounds for my 45 and given a grease gun as my t.o. weapons. Just for those not in the know, my grease gun was not for lubing jeeps, but a small 45 caliber machine gun that actually does resemble a grease gun – thus, the name, grease gun. We were all to find out what the excitement was a few hours later when the Captain announced over the intercom that the Red-Chinese had crossed the Mekong River and DMZ into Thailand. Thus, around two o'clock in the morning we were met approximately thirty to forty miles off the coast of Thailand, in the Gulf of Phnom Penn, in the South China Sea by a fleet of junks. Averaging about twenty to thirty men per junk, we loaded supplies and ammunition, and under the cover of darkness, stole silently up the Mekong River. We eventually set up camp just outside of Udorn, Thailand and from there, joining up with New Zealand Special Forces, made numerous reconnaissance and propaganda patrols into various villages in and out of the country. Places we shouldn't have necessarily been that were not acknowledged by the USA. Assigned as a forward observer I did some intelligence work such as authenticating maps and writing out daily reports on my observations of the villages and people there. Again, what I saw was a poor people, sick, uneducated and living a tortured existence. One never knows just how fat and good we live until we see how the other half lives. Even the miserable existence spent in prison where I wrote most of this book would be a Christmas wish of paradise for some of the people I've seen in Korea, Japan, Thailand and Vietnam. The faces of the children and their parents would tear you apart as you would watch them gather around our garbage cans to literally fight over our scraps like mad dogs.

During one of our many patrols, we chanced upon a small community in the middle of the jungle. We had been out for about a week and this was the forth or fifth village we came across. There were about twenty of us and my primary job was to authenticate the maps I had of the area. We also had a corpsman along who freely distributed penicillin and other much needed drugs to the people there.

There was a photographer, who helped to record our reconnaissance mission, for the "Stars and Stripes" newspaper. He even managed to get my picture in one issue as I interviewed one of the village elders.

At any rate, while we were in this particular village dispensing the appropriate propaganda, an ancient old fellow approached us and wondered if there was anything we could do about the big toe on his left foot. The thing was swollen to at least two and a half times its normal size and infected terribly. A quick diagnosis by the corpsman determined that the toe would have to be amputated. We tried to explain that we were not equipped to perform such an operation but the old man would have none of it. "If it has to go, it has to go, and do it now", he pleaded. The corpsman figured that with the infection, as bad as it was, the old guy probably wouldn't live very long anyway if left untreated so he consented to do it. Thus, sitting on the side of the road in the middle of the village the operation was about to begin. It was requested by the doc that I assist in this operation. So, after establishing a perimeter with my men I was given a quick course in which surgical instrument was which. The operation began and very quickly the toe was removed without the benefit of any anesthetic what-so-ever. The ancient old man just sat there quietly watching as we removed his toe chewing on whatever drug he had, probably beetle nut, which had kept him alive so far.

Suddenly, shots began to ring out and all hell broke loose. Grabbing a stack of gauze we slapped it on the end of the severed toe, quickly wrapped it up with tape and were off to find out what was up. A few more shots and I had the radio man call in the helicopters to pick us up. Technically, we were only there in an advisory capacity and not allowed to engage in any armed conflict. A few of our men did open fire and managed to chase whoever was firing at us away. He even left his gun behind which was an old French muzzle loading rifle. Then, just as suddenly, we were being fired on from another direction, and we quickly retreated to a small clearing at the edge of the village where we setup a smoke signal for the choppers that were arriving to pick us up. How those pilots got in and out of those little holes in the jungle is beyond me, but they did it, thank God, and we were off to safety.

At that particular time of the conflict the so-called enemy did not have very sophisticated weapons. It was all about bows and arrows, spears, booby traps, assorted small arms and homemade bombs. One of their favorite tricks was to blow up our latrines which made one very nervous when he had to go to the bathroom. This in turn only made us some very uptight and constipated Marines. More than once I was close enough to have shredded pieces of toilet paper and assorted crap rain down on me from a blast. I might add that I don't recall ever using one of these latrines for that very reason and choose to fertilize the jungle the old fashioned way.

Other incidents that took place at that time which had a sobering effect as to the seriousness of the situation involved public beatings and executions. Located in a large tent at the edge of the jungle next to our tent city the Thai officials would interrogate all those who were suspected of being communists or communist sympathizers. Such interrogations could often be heard throughout the camp and usually ended with a gun being placed to the head of the accused, and the killing or beating of them in full view of us Marines. Such public executions were soon stopped though, when still not hardened to the realities of the situation a group of Marines jumped on two Thai policemen who were brutally clubbing a nine year old boy to death with their Billy-clubs. Henceforth, it was ordered that all executions would be carried out in the jungle away from where we were camped.

Even though the conflict in this part of the world had not yet reached the sophisticated stages of weaponry that it was to eventually evolve to; it was apparently threatening enough to cause at least three men in our battalion to shoot themselves. I was witness to two of these men's actions as one shot his foot off and another put the barrel of his rifle to his calf. This was supposed to treat the victims, or should I say cowards, to a one way ticket back home and safety though I dare say not before a stop at the local brig and the receipt of a Dishonorable Discharge. While in Asia, I lived a pretty free wheeling, fast, loose and sometimes dangerous life, but also an educational one. Needless to say, this was the start of the Vietnam War, but luckily I got out before it really took hold.

Prior to our leaving Udorn, Thailand, what was left of our battalion was gathered together in a large open area where we were greeted by the King and Queen of Thailand. After reviewing the troops and shaking hands with several of us they gave each and every one of us a fifth of whisky and a carton of cigarettes to take home with us. I might also add that Queen Sirkrit was a truly beautiful woman, as were many of the Thai/Siamese ladies I met there.

The infamous "smoker" with Army Sgt. Jones, only served to put me into the ring every time a fight card was scheduled. The next fight took place aboard the USS Navarro. I KO'd the Navy's heavyweight champ, also in the third round, and also required several of the Navy's finest to pull me off of him.

My final fight for the Marine Corps took place at Udorn, Thailand. It was a festive affair with Ambassadors, General Simpson and other foreign dignitaries attending. I was to fight the all-service heavyweight champion and the fifth ranked heavyweight contender in the world, Clarence "John" Henry. I was not entirely pleased with the person who entered my name in this contest, but since he outranked me, my

CO, there was nothing I could do about it. So, when the main event took place, I was standing in my corner of the ring staring across at the biggest black man I had ever seen in my life. When the bell rang, I attacked quickly and actually got through his defense and hit him with everything I had right on the button. He didn't even blink an eye. I did it again. Still I didn't faze him. One final attempt on my part, and he just looked at me like I was some sort of troublesome fly. He then commenced to beat me unmercifully across the ring and back again, until the referee saw fit to save my life and stop it. Never have I seen such a science at its peak. He was a true professional of his craft and I couldn't help but admire his skill as he raised welts all over my forehead and face. I can say this; he still never knocked me down or out. But laying helplessly against the ropes as he pummeled me the ref seen fit to call it a TKO and that was the end of the one sided fight. That evening Clarence and I spent a wild night on the town together in the local bars and brothels and that little event capped the end of my boxing career.

Another form of entertainment we used to indulge ourselves in was rickshaw races. Actually, they were called Pedi-cabs. A form of a rickshaw, only instead of the coolie running in between the carrying handles, he attached the front end of a bicycle and peddled us around. That's called progress. We would sometimes get two or three of us heavy Marines in these things and encourage the driver to race another cab through the middle of the streets by offering more money to him if he won.

On one particular evening I was by myself in one of these cabs racing against a fiend of mine in another cab. Well, as could only happen to me as we were tearing down through the middle of town, a huge mongrel dog darted out from nowhere in front of my driver who hit him squarely in the side, jackknifed the wheel, and over we went, with me skidding along on my face and hands. I swear, I have to be the only guy in the world to total a rickshaw.

After thirteen months my tour of duty in the Orient came to an end and I was on my way back to the United States. Catching a 707 out of Los Angeles I flew to Chicago and took a train from there to Lansing. A thirty-day leave at home and then it was off to Quantico, Virginia just outside of Washington DC where the Marine Corps assigned me to a guard company. I became a prison guard at the interservice brig situated right next to the Federal Bureau of Investigation, (FBI) Academy. A military prison, especially a "red line" brig run by the Navy and Marine Corps makes Jackson Prison look like a vacation spot at Disneyworld. Although, thank God, I understand that red line brigs are no longer in existence. To be sentenced to such an institution, at that time, was pure hell. These guys upon entrance were subjected to total humiliation and degradation. Each and every prisoner was subjected to a total strip search every time they exited or left the prison on work gangs and again randomly throughout the day and night. Still, at that time, which totally baffled me, we found contraband every day in their cells and on their person.

Every Thursday evening, armed with tooth brushes, they were required to scrub down their dorms top to bottom. The "Hole", should you be unlucky enough to be sent there for some infraction of the rules, was just that; a dark, black hole, no daylight and no light what-so-ever, unless a guard was present to check on you. Breakfast consisted of black coffee. Lunch time was a half head of cabbage and a tin of water. Dinner was bread and water and sometimes, if the prisoner was good, some peanut butter on the bread which was at the guard's discretion. That's it, no variation.

I certainly did not care for this type of duty, and being close now to the end of my enlistment I was offered the job of a Boy Scout counselor in Woodbridge, Virginia. There, for three months I taught Boy Scouts all over the eastern part of the United States how to shoot, and the ins and outs of gun safety. We had both a target and skeet range and this duty was one of the most enjoyable jobs I've ever had while in the service.

Also, during this time I retook my GED test once again in Lansing according to the specifications of the Lansing School Board. Now I was officially graduated from JW Sexton and my name included in a graduating class. In a surprise visit my parents and sister, Carol came to Virginia to give me my diploma and we spent the weekend together in Washington DC. We visited many of the historical sites and my sister and I walked down the stairs of the Washington monument, a chore I recommend only for the physically fit. I didn't think we'd ever run out of stairs and reach the bottom.

I received an honorable discharge from the Marine Corps on September 23, 1963 and returned home to Lansing. During my stint in the Marine Corps I had often hitch-hiked back and forth across the country from California to Michigan. That in itself was an education in America and its people. They were wonderful experiences that unfortunately do not exist today. Hitch-hiking used to be a popular form of travel for many. But times have changed and such modes of travel are now dangerous for both rider and driver alike.

CHAPTER 4

The Real World following the Marine Corps

Once home, I found an apartment to live in and got a job in order to finance the purchase of a new car. The first job I took was as a taxi driver for the Courtesy Cab Company. That was another interesting job where I met many strange and nice people, but only held for a short time, due to the fact that I was involved in a pretty nasty accident with one of the cabs.

The accident involved a passenger I was taking to Sparrow Hospital. He was going to get a cast removed from his arm that he had worn for the past six weeks. He was very excited about that prospect and it was all he could talk about on the trip there. As I passed the Armory coming up Marshall Street I approached a traffic light that was in the process of changing to red. But I wasn't aware of that fact, due to the fact that my passenger had chosen that particular moment to pay what was owed on the meter. Just as I was turning back around from receiving that payment is when I noticed the light changing. Well, I was driving one of those big slow Checker cars, a favorite of cab companies for some reason, so when I made the decision to put the peddle to the metal there was just not enough guts in the old girl to get across the intersection in time.

As my luck would have it, a little Chevy II was crossing the same intersection, at the same time, in the opposite direction. Somehow it hit me exactly right and flipped that huge Checker high enough into the air to come down on top of a mailbox located on the corner of the street. When the world finally stopped spinning I found myself in the back seat. My only thought then was to get the hell out of there as fast as I could. So, I climbed out the back window to safety. My next concern of course, was for my passenger. But I couldn't find him. He was nowhere to be seen in the car and he wasn't anywhere outside of the car, that I could see. I almost started to panic wondering where he could be when I began to hear some low moans coming from underneath the car. Only his head was sticking out, just off the curb into the street, the car balancing precariously on his chest and the curb. His pitiful moans of "help me", sprang me into action, the adrenaline surging, for should the car continue to roll it would surely crush his skull. Reaching down, and with new found strength I tried to lift the car off from him, or to at least hold it steady so it wouldn't roll any further. By that time, a couple of school kids came by and proceeded to help me in this endeavor. Together, we did manage to roll that monster off my passenger to an upright position so that the arriving ambulance attendants could reach him. They also took me to the hospital to check for injuries and found that I didn't have so much as a scratch on me. Not so for my passenger who now had practically every bone in his body broken. All I could think of as they rolled his pitiful moaning body past me on a stretcher was of how happy he was to be coming here to get the cast taken off his arm. Now, his entire body would be in a cast. I certainly hope the insurance company made it worthwhile for him.

My next job was with Central Advertising, an outdoor advertising agency that puts up and maintains all those signs you see along the highways, and in and out, and on the tops of buildings. I started out as one who puts up posters, then to sign erection and finally to the maintenance department.

It was in the winter of 1963 that I met Pauline. This was the time of folk music, beatniks and rock and roll. On one particular night I hitched a ride with some guy I met in a bar out to another bar at Lake Lansing. While getting a beer from the bar I turned around and almost bumped into one of the most exotic and beautiful ladies I'd ever seen. She was dressed all in black from head to toe. Her hair was long, black and lovely and hung down to her waist. Her face was classic, haughty, snobbish, earthy and beautiful. I had to meet her. So, I tried one of my more cleaver lines; "Hi there, my name is..." "I know who you are," she answered, before I finished. Well, needless to say, I was caught by surprise and dumbfounded by this beautiful creature. I was pretty sure my glowing fame couldn't have preceded me here because I didn't have any. I believe she teased me for quite awhile before she let me know how she knew me, which of course was from my early days of dating the Michigan State University Sophomore, a couple of my then teenage friends and the home of my uncle Mel.

We spent the evening visiting, drinking and dancing together. It was Pauline's girl friend who eventually drove us back to the city where we stopped for something to eat and eventually home. I was living at the YMCA at this time due to another auto accident that I was involved in when I spun out on an icy patch of road and slammed into a telephone pole and had to live someplace a little less expensive to pay some bills I owed. Besides working eight to ten hours a day at Central Advertising, I also worked at a friend's gas station from six to ten each evening pumping gas and washing cars. Ah, the days of full service gas stations.

When I dropped Pauline off that night I did manage to get her phone number. Because I was so excited and infatuated with this lady she didn't have to use too many of her wily ways to have me panting in her ear over the phone the next day asking for a date. She accepted and it was a date for dinner and dancing beginning at eight o'clock. I took off early from work, dashed home and got all slicked up. I ran out to my new old car and turned the key. Nothing happened. I ran to the phone. "Hi, Pauline, I may be a little late. My car won't start." Nine o'clock. "Hi, Pauline please don't worry. Just a little car trouble, but I'll be there soon." Ten o'clock. Oh Lord, why me? Here I've got this fantastic chick and my damn car won't start. Panic time. "Uh, hi Pauline. Hang in there. Be there soon." I ended up calling my friend Sam at the gas station who came to pick both me and my car up and tow it back to the station. By now it was Eleven-thirty pm. "Hi, Pauline. Told ya I'd make it. Are ya ready to go out?" Luckily I didn't get to see the look on her face when I escorted her out of the house in her dinner dress to be confronted by the sight of a huge red Texaco fuel gas truck. When I look back on it the poor girl must have been just as crazy about me, otherwise, why else would she still have agreed to go out with me that night at that late hour, ushered around in such luxurious transportation? We ended up going to an all-night restaurant, called the Trio, where she sat quietly and watched me eat a double order of eggs, ham and potatoes. Hell, I worked up an appetite just getting to her. And that's how I met Pauline. Our second date wasn't any more successful than the first I'm afraid. Pauline offered to fix dinner for me at her place this time, so I of course accepted. I did get there on time and the dinner was fabulous. After the dishes were cleaned and put away we turned down the lights and celebrated by putting on some romantic mood music on the record player. All was going perfectly well until we decided to dance. I would really show her my stuff now. My moves would have made Fred Astaire envious until we reached the end of the song and I attempted to end with a dip. To this day I'm not sure how it happened, but somehow Pauline got her foot twisted and as I bent her back there was a loud snapping noise. Yup, I just broke her ankle. I was batting a thousand so far. But luckily she took it all in stride and didn't tell me to get lost.

Things fortunately progressed from that point and we saw each other often and at every chance we got. We were falling in love with each other and working together to save up enough money to get me out of debt and put enough aside to fulfill the plans we were making together of marriage. Interspersed in these plans were frequent arguments with our parents, who were exerting pressure on both of us, for and against the marriage.

In fact, Pauline's father actually threatened me once with a gun on his front porch as to the honorability of my intentions toward his daughter. Remember, he was a full-blooded orthodox Italian and you just don't string their daughter's along. Although that was not my intention, his threat only helped to bring out the stubborn German in me.

When I first met my future father-in-law, Paul Amedeo, "Harry" DeRose, I was fresh out of the Marine Corps, in perfect physical condition and afraid of nothing and no one. I had been dating his daughter Pauline for about three months now and also unaware of his connection with those folks in organized crime. Thus, upon our first meeting, when I knocked on his door to pickup Pauline for a date, he answered with a small automatic pistol in his hand and asking what my intentions were with his daughter' in a very threatening manner.

I responded by telling him, "first, that if he didn't put the gun away, I would shove it up his ass, and furthermore, my intentions were none of his business, since both Pauline and I were adults, and what would happen, would happen on our schedule and not his." Before the conversation escalated any further both Pauline and her mother came to the door and attempted to calm the situation down, with Lucille, his wife pulling him back inside the house.

Although my intentions were to eventually ask for Pauline's hand in marriage, I deliberately held off for another three months before doing so because I was not going to be pressured into a marriage by anyone. Harry, as he liked to be called, owned a strip club named, Amedeo's and was the only such club in Lansing at that time. It was a very successful establishment, about a block away from the capitol, and would be frequented by Senators, Legislators, Judges, Lawyers and people; mostly men, from all walks of life.

Once Pauline and I were married, another three months later, Harry's attitude towards me changed immediately. Our first outing together was him taking me to the race track in Hazel Park, Michigan. I had a whopping ten dollars on me to bet with. I am not a gambler. Once at the track, he told me to bet the entire ten on the daily double, and on the numbers he gave to me. Well, I did bet the numbers he gave me on those horses, but again, not being a gambler, I only bet two dollars. Hell, I didn't want to be broke on the first two races already. At that time, I didn't know that I wasn't really gambling, because if I did what he told me to do, I wouldn't/couldn't lose. Of course, those numbers/horses won and instead of $5,000.00 in my pocket, I had won a whopping $500.00. Damn, that was almost a month's wages back then for me. I was in seventh heaven. He now asked me to bet the entire five thousand on this next horse. When I told him what I did he just frowned and shook his head and said, "Well then, bet the five hundred on this horse." "What are you, nuts?" I thought to myself. I came with ten dollars and now have five hundred. I'm a winner. I'm happy. So, I bet a whole ten dollars this time. Yup, the horse won. Well, needless to say, Harry was a bit disappointed with me that day, but I still came home with enough money to make a substantial down payment on our first house.

Going to the race track now became a frequent routine. I was designated as the driver to and from the track, which was kind of fun, sitting behind the wheel of his big Lincoln Continental Town Car. We were definitely VIP status at the track, as we were the only car that could park at the front entrance and not be hasseled.

I was later to learn that Joe Zerelli was the owner of the track. Joe, pretty much ran the Midwestern families back then which were known better as the LaCosa Nostra, or Mafia by most people. In all our trips to the track I never once saw who Harry's contact was there. He would position me on the ground floor ramp and at his command would call out or flash me a number to bet on, and then I would run to the $50.00 window as fast as I could and bet as much as I could until the bell shut off all betting. Of course, we would win - all ten races - and return home with more money than I had ever seen in my life. We would then race back to Lansing, usually behind the Governor's limo, so we could exceed the speed limit with some degree of safety. Then Harry would make a call to the president of Michigan National Bank, who would then open the bank and deposit the winnings for him.

Eventually, Harry would end up owning what was later to be referred to as the "sin block" in Lansing. Strip clubs, gay bars and adult book stores. That block would eventually be torn down to what is now called the Oldsmobile ball park.

But, back to the races. There was a time the track would run what was called the "Twin Double". A bettor would have to win two races in a row, and then turn in his ticket and correctly pick the last two races in order to win a huge jackpot. The odds of a bettor to win all four races in a row were obviously very high. The smallest pot I ever seen was around five thousand dollars, but the majority of them generally ran into the fifty to a hundred thousand plus dollar range.

There were times when Harry would have myself and Pauline station ourselves by the ticket windows and as the players would try to exchange their first two winning tickets for the last two numbers we would offer them fifty or a hundred dollars for the tickets. Not a bad offer, when all they had invested was two dollars. Now, if we could purchase enough winning tickets we could pick a couple of favorites in the 9th race and then run all the numbers in the 10th race. It never failed. We always won.

One again, we were winning large sums of money and Pauline and I, or whoever else was working for us, would run from one window to another to cash in the tickets in an effort to avoid any IRS people.

Eventually, the Attorney General of Michigan, Frank Kelly, smelled something fishy was going on at Hazel Park Raceway, and a subsequent investigation ensued, which resulted in the demise of the "Twin Double" and eventually the forced sale of the Hazel Park Race Track.

"Argosy" Magazine did a short story and profile on Harry and the track back then but other than the selling off of the property, no other charges were filed that I'm aware of. But, it was a good haul for a short time. I have often wondered what Harry did for the "family" that returned to him such huge winnings.

Harry did like to gamble. I know that a lot of the money he won at Hazel Park he would take over to Canada at the Windsor Race Track and bet on the trotters and would lose more than he would win. He also bet a lot on cards and various other sporting events. Harry and the Family also had a lot of people in their clutches when it came to gambling. I do know that my father-in-law reported and took his orders from one Joe Corey who he would meet with from time to time and they would set up more than a few high stakes card games in both the Lansing and Jackson areas and where some of the more prominent sports figures of our time would fall into their clutches. On more than one occasion he would hand me a small 32 caliber pistol and send me off on a mission to collect money from one or more folks who forgot to pay off on a debt. Usually this would take place at was then called a "Blind Pig" in an upstairs building on Allegan Street in Lansing. In that way I could always pick up a few more dollars for my family so long as I kept it quiet from members of the family, especially the wife and mother-in-law. Fortunately, I was always pretty lucky in my collections, and never ran into any serious problems. All involved knew full well who they were dealing with and pulling back on my coat jacket to reveal the butt of a gun usually silenced any objections. One of the people in the Families clutches which stands out, was the 30 game winner for the Detroit Tigers, Denny McClain, who ran up a tidy sum that eventually ruined him. Always felt bad about that one. I don't believe poor Denny has ever recovered from his dealings with that Family and hope by now he's worked out those problems. There were also several other well known sports figures caught in the family's clutches at that time which is no secret, like Detroit Lions Tackler, Alex Karras and Dick "Night Train" Lane.

During my stint behind the walls of Jackson Prison, I was privy to meet one of the more famous members of the Detroit family. Vito Giacalone was a reputed capo in the La Casa Nostra. He was a stocky, rotund man, who could play the part of anyone's kindly old grandfather, unlike his steely-eyed brother, Anthony, "Tony Jack" Giacalone. But, together they ruled Detroit with an iron fist. Tony, the more vicious of the two is who Jimmy Hoffa was to meet on the day of his disappearance.

Vito, would walk around the prison yard with an entourage of wanna-be body guards and hanger-ons, and he would engage in various gaming and gambling events. He would flaunt his wealth, at times by buying all the ice cream in the prison store and giving out as many pints to as many inmates as possible, until the store ran out. A great treat on hot summer prison days to be sure.

Of course, there was always the code of Omerta that dominates the family and in various little parlor meetings around the yard, the name of Hoffa would eventually creep into the conversation. When that would happen it would get a threatening stare or worse from his real body guard at that time, a Pete Katranis. Katranis was a very scary person, and I must admit, the only person in my life that really in fact did scare me a little. But, as I've learned in life there is always someone scarier around the corner as Katranis was to find out not too much later when they found his body stuffed in the trunk of his Cadillac at Detroit Metro Airport.

But, let's get back to the story. Although Vito would never encourage such conversations, he would remark about how stupid the FBI and other law enforcement agencies were that they couldn't figure out what had happened to Hoffa. Everything was right there in front of their eyes yet they couldn't seem to figure it out. Even if they did, there wasn't much they could do about it, because there is no body to be found. He's pushing up daisies alright, but only in the truest sense of the word - as fertilizer. With the Family having an interest in the waste management business in Detroit, it should be obvious, right? But, I guess not as they keep looking and hoping they will find his remains. We've all heard the rumors that he was buried under third base at a major league stadium, he was buried in a cement corner stone of a large building, and more recently as everyone watched on TV as the FBI dug up an entire farm looking for him.

For at least thirty years the Detroit Family of the La Cosa Nostra

(LCN) was an extremely active criminal enterprise consisting of approximately 30 "made members" and between 200 and 300 associates, according to the FBI, of which Paul "Harry" Amedeo DeRose, my father-in law was one. Vito "Billy Jack" was the caretaker of the families gambling operations in Michigan and Ohio. As reported in Detroit's two major newspapers members are tightly bound through blood and marriage, making the organization extremely difficult to penetrate. Traditionally, this family has been involved in illegal gambling, loan sharking, money laundering, drug trafficking, and the infiltration of legitimate business. They have also maintained a strong relationship with Sicilian Mafia members operating in the Detroit area.

Jimmy P. Hoffa disappeared from the outside of the now-defunct Machus Red Fox restaurant at Telegraph and Maple in Bloomfield Township. He had gone there to meet with Anthony (Tony Jack) Giacalone, Vito's brother, of which both were Detroit Mafia bosses, and Tony Provenzano, a New Jersey Teamsters boss and Mafia associate.

Neither of these men ever showed up. Giacalone and Provenzano, who have since died, denied any meeting had been scheduled.

Investigators believe that Hoffa, 62, was picked up outside the restaurant and subsequently killed. Since the beginning, investigators have had evidence that Hoffa had been in a 1975 maroon Mercury Marquis Brougham driven by Chuckie O'Brien. O'Brien had borrowed the car from his friend Joey Giacalone, son of Anthony Gaicalone.

Investigators and Hoffa's family have long said that O'Brien, who had been taken in by Hoffa as a child was one of the few people who could persuade Hoffa to get into a car that day.

O'Brien told police that Hoffa was never in the car and that he was running errands. But police dogs, after sniffing clothing worn the day before he disappeared, found Hoffa's scent in the rear of the Mercury. FBI technicians found a single, three inch brown head of hair in the car that had "characteristics similar" to Hoffa's hair, according to law enforcement files obtained by The Detroit Free Press in 1992.

Not long ago the FBI had the hair tested, using the new DNA technology, against hair from Hoffa's hair brush. It matched.

A Bloomfield Hills attorney James Burdick, who represented O'Brien after Hoffa vanished, ridiculed the significance of the new DNA evidence, saying it doesn't add much to the case. It's objectively stupid to think O'Brien had anything to do with Hoffa's death, said

Burdick. He also said that O'Brien was too indiscreet to be trusted with such a high-profile killing. "He'd be the last guy in this nation you would want to know your secrets," Burdick said.

Still, legal experts and Hoffa Aficionados alike were fascinated by the latest turn in the mystery. "It calls Chuckie into question, obviously," said Arthur Sloane, author of the biography, "Hoffa." But legal experts who were interviewed were unanimous that the DNA match, without more evidence, was unlikely to put anyone behind bars. Lawyers have said O'Brien could offer any number of explanations for why Hoffa's hair turned up in the back seat of the car borrowed from Joe Giacalone. Just one of the many obstacles that prosecutors would face should they try to bring charges against O'Brien.

Hoffa had long standing ties to the Giacalone family and could have been in the car long before his disappearance. A strand of hair is easily lost from the scalp, and could have been transferred by someone who had come into contact with it. Even if prosecutors could prove Hoffa was in the car on that day, they would still need to show that O'Brien, or any in an endless cast of mob characters, was responsible for Hoffa's death. This statement was from an article in the Detroit Free Press on September, 8, 2001 by David Ashenfelter and Jim Schaffer.

Just before he died, a Frank Sheeran, nick-named, "The Irishman" was one of a handful of FBI suspects in Hoffa's murder. Sheeran was close to Hoffa and confessed to Charles Brandt that he killed Hoffa. According to Sheeran, Chuckie O'Brien drove Hoffa, Sheeran and Sal Briguglio to a house in Detroit. Hoffa and Sheeran went into the house and the other two men drove off. Sheeran says he shot Hoffa twice behind the right ear. After the murder, Sheeran says he left the house and was told Hoffa was cremated. This from the book by Brandt, "I Heard You Paint Houses".

This brings us to Peter Vitale, father in-law to Joseph Barbara Jr., who was also in prison at the same time as Vito "Billy Jack" Giacalone and also one who followed Vito around the yard constantly looking over his shoulder and scared to death that he was going to be shived (stabbed) to death at any moment. At any rate, Mr. Vitale was the co-owner of Central Sanitation Services in Detroit which was suspected in the past as being a dumping ground for other suspected "Hits"."Bozzi" as Peter Vitale was often referred to also served as the underboss to Joe Zerilli. I would like to add one more name to the list of Hoffa's disappearance. Peter Katranis. Not a family member, and which carries no guilt for any assassination since he was not a family member and therefore not one who would be totally protected or traced back to the Family. And once again, Hoffa, as intimated by the family and those I had chance to be around and associate with state rather freely that he was totally ground up and disposed of through Central Sanitation. There is no body to be found. I know it's a hard pill to swallow for many who would like to find a body, which in turn would initiate an investigation and hopefully bring new answers to a long lasting mystery. But, I'm afraid you're all going to have to accept the inevitable. There is no body to be found.

So, why was it necessary to eliminate Hoffa? Hoffa who was the head of the Teamsters Union was a powerful leader and controlled many if not all of the trucks on the road and beloved by all who worked for him. He was also in control of the Teamsters pension fund. After many years of trying to convict Hoffa, then United States Attorney General, Robert Kennedy finally succeeded in doing so only for Hoffa's sentence to be commuted by President Nixon. At that point in time Hoffa was in good standing with the Family and they both used each other to their advantage. Once Hoffa was convicted, Frank Fitzsimmons was appointed the new head of the Teamsters Union. Now out, and eventually off parole, Hoffa wanted to regain control of the Teamsters. Thus, he declared his intention to run for the presidency of the Brotherhood of the International Brotherhood of Teamsters. But now the Family who had worked well with Hoffa in the past wasn't so sure they wanted him back due to the fact that Hoffa wasn't so sure he wanted to be associated with the Family and have to cow-tow to their every wish. The Family thought that Frank Fitzsimmons was a lot easier to deal with than Hoffa, and they wanted Hoffa to remain retired. Fitzsimmons and the Giacalones were now good friends, and with him in charge had easier access to the Teamsters pension fund and wanted to expand their gambling empire into Nevada. Even though they had a controlling interest in the Alladin and Frontier Hotels and Casinos, the heat was on and they wanted to expand into Laughlin, Nevada south of Las Vegas to escape the watchful eye of the gaming commission.

Thus, The Edgewater Hotel and Casino were created and the small town of Laughlin was on the map, allegedly financed by Teamster pension money. With Hoffa back in control, which was very likely due to his popularity with the Teamsters, it was just too much of a risk to take. Hoffa fought his way up the ranks the hard way and not a person easily threatened or scared, and would probably have told the Giacalones to go pound sand. He was not about to take the chance of going back to prison, and with an ego the size of Mt Everest was not about to take orders from anyone. So the simplest and easiest conclusion was to eliminate the problem, and the rest is history.

Well, back to the marriage which finally came off. Pauline and I were officially married on August 29, 1964 at St. Mary's. It wasn't a large wedding, by Italian standards, due to the fact that we were married to soon after the death of Pauline's uncle, Patsy Coscarelli. Also, I don't think my parents and family were in favor or supportive of the marriage. To be perfectly honest I was a bit disappointed about the way the reception came off. But, the wedding itself was beautiful, and Pauline looked absolutely gorgeous in her traditional white gown.

During our courtship we saved enough money for a down payment on a house on 317 South Holmes Street. Thanks to her father's monetary help via the race track winnings I later converted it into a two-family dwelling and for extra income we rented out the upstairs apartment.

Our wedding reception was held in that house before we packed our bags and in my little Ford Falcon, now repaired since our first date, we were off on our honeymoon to Dallas, Texas and a visit with one of Pauline's girl friends.

It was a fun trip. We took our time and picnicked and stopped at various places along the way. In Texas, we stayed at Pauline's friend's apartment. We swam, visited a few nightclubs, including Jack Ruby's, the Carousel, a bar pretty much setup the same way as Pauline's father's nightclub, which was called, Amedeos, at that time. Jack Ruby, as history shall record was the one who eventually shot and killed Lee Harvey Oswald, who was accused of the assassination of President John F. Kennedy. We visited that historic spot also. It was also a working honeymoon in an effort to try and put Ruby's girls on the circuit. Actually, Ruby's bar, the Carousel was a second story bar with the stage in the middle. Dallas, being a dry town at that time prohibited the purchase of alcohol in a bar or nightclub. There, only the set-ups were provided so we brought our own bottle and settled back to watch the show and girls dance. We also were to meet with the manager, who I have no clue who he was at that time, and we tried to set him and the girls up on the circuit. In other words, the dancers would travel to Chicago, Detroit, Lansing, Toledo, etc., with a four-week stay at each place. Thus; the nightclubs would not have to have the same dancers for an extended period of time and therefore, variety.

After about a week, we were on our way back to Lansing. I went back to work at Central Advertising and Pauline tended to the household chores. I've always thought she was a fabulous cook, and with my passion for Italian cooking it wasn't hard for her to keep me happy in that department.

Prior to our marriage, Pauline was already pregnant with our first child. A child we both looked forward to with anticipation. She went through the usual feelings of inadequacy and worry that I understand most women go through at such times. But, we weathered it through, and on March 12, 1965 our first little girl was born. I fulfilled the fatherly duty of pacing the hospital floors back and forth, back and forth until the birth, which was not an easy one for Pauline, but all considered, certainly worth the effort. Our daughter was beautiful and healthy. We were two very happy and proud parents and very much in love with our new little girl.

Our baby was always a feisty little thing, always full of energy and with a terrific set of lungs. If there was something bothering her, she always let us know it in no uncertain terms. But, in quieter times we had a lot of fun together. I remember well our wrestling matches together, chasing her across the floor, playing hide and seek and our famous pillow fights. She had a special kind of bubbling giggle that used to bring tears of joy to me every time I heard it.

While I was working at Central Advertising I began working with a young guy that I was to train in the poster business. We were partners on a sign route and worked well together. Often we would complete our work early and return to our house where we sat around, relaxed, collected overtime and enjoyed a beer or two. On one occasion we stopped at my parent's house for a cup of coffee and that is where this fellow met my sister, Judy. Not expecting visitors, she had just awakened, and came upon us in a shabby robe that looked like it had been rescued from the Salvation Army throw away pile and hair that looked like it had gone through a war with a mix-master and lost. Well, needless to say, something sparked between them as they began to date and in a few short months they were engaged to be married and in fact were eventually married.

After Pauline and I were married I dropped the part-time job at the Texaco gas station and worked exclusively for Central Advertising with the exception of about four months during the summer when I helped to tend bar and bounce for Pauline's father at his nightclub. Amedeos, at that time, was the only nightclub in Lansing that featured live entertainment in the form of strippers. Dancing to recorded music the girls would strip down to pasties and G-strings, with the occasional inebriated lass taking things all the way to the buff to the delight and applause of the predominately male audience. Amedeos was a popular and financially successful business that catered to all levels of the social structure as I stated earlier. There were college students and doctors, lawyers and judges, comingling with derelicts and low-lifers and all forms of conventioneers. It was an interesting job to be sure.

The girls that danced there would normally only stay for about three or four weeks before traveling on to another city on their circuit. But, as they passed through I was to meet several that left a lasting impression.

One such girl was a tall blonde named Carol, from Chicago, who took a particular liking to Pauline and me. She was a very statuesque and beautiful girl who we invited to our house for dinner. It just so happened that my parents picked that night to stop by and needless to say it was an evening to remember as my parents tried to appear worldly and relate to this creature of another world. In contrast, poor Carol tried her best to act dignified and not converse in the typical language of the street which she was so used to.

But Carol had a heart of gold, and knowing how Pauline and I were struggling to make ends meet, she suggested that we bring some of the stuffed animals to the bar that I had won at a church carnival a week earlier and she would sell them for us. And sell them she did. She must have sold each stuffed animal, a total of five of them, at least two or three times a day. Displayed prominently on the bar, she would go from customer to customer dressed in her scanty costume pleading to each leering gentleman as she went, that she just had to have that stuffed teddy bear or stuffed rabbit for her poor little daughter who she had to leave back in Chicago. Of course, no such child existed, but by collecting anywhere from one to ten dollars per customer, depending upon who wanted to impress her the most, she was able to buy the two or three fuzzy creatures several times a night. Once she had bought it, and after the customers she had put the touch on left the bar, she would give us the stuffed animal back and we would eventually resell it to her once again that night. She would never accept a dime for her efforts and gave all the profits to Pauline and I, which at twenty dollars a crack was a pretty good piece of change per night. She was a very special lady and I'm sure Pauline and I will never forget her.

Another incident that took place at the nightclub involved a college student who refused to show me his identification. After several minutes of trying to reason with him, that if he couldn't prove he was twenty-one, he would not be served and have to leave the bar. He was determined to show off for his three buddies and force me to throw him out. So, if that is what he wanted, then I was certainly not going to disappoint him. Quickly grabbing him by his ears I slammed his face to the table and spun around behind him where I locked both of his arms in mine and proceeded to push him out through the bar. He, unfortunately, picked the farthest table from the entrance, so it took all of my dexterity to maneuver him through the crowded tables without causing too much of a disturbance to the other patrons, as he tried to fight me all the way. By the time I was halfway to the door his three buddies decided it was time to exhibit some form of comradeship and started forward to offer some help to him.

While all this commotion was going on there was a little Puerto Rican on stage who went by the name of "Jet", who was trying to perform her best version of "Salome and the Seven Veils". Well, these young hooligans were just creating a heck of a disturbance during her act which did not set well with her. So, seeing the three companions on their way to help, she leaped off the stage and grabbed up two beer bottles from a customer's table which she began to swing threateningly over her head between me and the on-coming cavalry, and in her best five foot one inch John Wayne stance, and language that would have made even Linda Lovelace blush, she held the reluctant heroes at bay as I proceeded to drive Joe College out the door. Unfortunately I missed the door on a couple of tries and slammed his head into the door jam. Once I got him out to the street I figured that would be the end of it and turned around to re-enter the bar. As I did, I made the fatal mistake of turning my back on him. He came after me and grabbing my shoulder, turned me around and succeeded in hitting me in the nose which caused it to bleed. Well, this little victory just turned his world into a joyful place to live and he started to dance around expressing his glee at the damage he inflicted on me until I countered with a little exhibition of my own in the ancient art of karate upon his little smeller, which was promptly shattered into a bright red splotch. The fight suddenly went out of him as he fell to the pavement and now with his reassembled band of scholars, hobbled off to the prosecutors' office where, would you believe; he tried to press charges against me. Of course, the prosecutor helped in furthering the young man's education and the matter was finished.

Although I liked working for Central Advertising I wanted to get out from behind the wheel of a truck and construction work and enter the sales department. Several times I approached the management about these possibilities but I was always put off with promises of later. Discouraged, I answered a blind ad in the local newspaper and accepted a job with Max Curtis Ford as a used car salesman. After almost two years with Central Advertising, I made more at Curtis Ford my first month as a salesman working only four hours a day than I did at Central working for two months at ten hours a day. Ford Motor Institute had an excellent sales training school at the time, and after graduating from that I became a top salesman in the company. I enjoyed the work immensely.

Within a few short months as their top salesperson there came a time at Curtis Ford when a gentleman who owned a used car lot called, Crain's Motors, approached me with an offer to manage his car lot. He guaranteed me a thousand dollars a month plus commission which was an excellent income at that time, in 1964-65. Plus, there was an added benefit as the lot was just down the block from our house. So, the offer appealed to me and I accepted it. I was soon to make more money than I ever did in my life. I helped to build his one lot into four separate used car lots around the city and we became one of the top independent dealers in the city, even outselling Story Oldsmobile at one point. Story Oldsmobile was the largest volume dealer in Lansing at that time.

During this time, into my first year of marriage with Pauline I had many good moments. But, we also had some stormy times together. When you marry an Italian you marry the entire family and therein existed many of our problems. But, to place the blame on any one person or thing is impossible. I feel we must share that problem equally. We both could have done things differently, more thoughtfully and much more caringly. We were living too freely and irresponsibly. There became a financial problem among all the rest facing us. I became dissatisfied with my job at Crains and left it to go to work for Jack Dykstra Ford. I was to only work there for about three weeks before the worst time of our lives descended upon us.

Ironically, I think Pauline and I were beginning to work out our problems together. We grew a little closer together in those final weeks and it was during one of these close encounters that the twins were conceived. I know Pauline and I both remember the exact moment it happened. It was a moment of great tenderness and love. Sure enough, nine months later they made their appearance into this world. But prior to their arrival, something happened that was to shatter our lives forever. On July 11, 1965, I was arrested for the murder of Mrs. Betty Reynolds.

CHAPTER 5

The Prison Years

The twelve years that I spent in prison were not entirely a waste. I did manage to complete a few programs, learn a few trades and helped to update the prison system in Michigan. When you first enter prison you are assigned to an area called RDC (Reception Diagnostic Center) and you remain there for at least 30 days before you are allowed to enter the prison population. You are run through a battery of psychological tests to see if you're a mental case or not and where you would best be suited for placement within the prison system. Within the second day of my arrival and once assigned a cell number I was called to the "Top Six" area, which is considered the mental ward of the prison. "Oh shit" I thought, "not already. I hadn't even taken a test yet." But to my surprise I was greeted by an old friend of mine who was serving a life sentence for murder in the Lansing area. Besides my case being much publicized and the majority of those in prison who follow such events, a lot of the guys knew pretty well that I was being railroaded. So, they sat me down and explained to me the ropes and the ins and outs of the prison system and how I should handle myself. I was immediately loaded up with cigarettes which were acknowledged to be the traditional bargaining currency in the joint. Also, I was given a sack full of snacks and goodies as well as a box of books. Hell, the first day in and here I was already doing better than any of the other guys in RDC. Fortunately, this immediately alerted all the rest of my fellow inmates in RDC that I had friends in here and probably shouldn't be one to mess with. When we had our few hours of yard time to walk and recreate they would come up to me and ask what was going on. I just played dumb which wasn't too hard because I really was. Thus, after all of my psychological testing I was eventually placed into "population" and sent to 2-Block where I would spend the first few years of my incarceration.

The first job I had while in prison was in the Academic School, where I went to work for Mr. Peter Benda, the head of the Closed Circuit Television (CCTV) Department. Why Benda was even employed there is beyond me. He was much too intelligent and progressive for the place. Prior to coming to Jackson, he was a director/producer for the National Educational Television (NET) network and had several documentaries to his credit. Needless to say, he only lasted a little over a year at the prison. But, before he left he taught me a lot about what goes on behind the scenes within television production and direction.

The one thing we were able to do together was to create a closed circuit television talk show throughout the prison. I served as host and interviewer for a program appropriately titled, "The Chair." On the program we would interview various prison officials and ask them questions that were sent in to us by the residents. We had great plans for the show and it soon became a big hit with the rest of the inmate population, although it was to last for only six tapings, I feel we did accomplish a lot by putting the various officials on the "hot seat", so to speak.

For instance, at this time, the only clothes being worn in the prison were brown work style uniforms. In an effort to save the state some money and to provide a little dignity and individualism back to the inmates we were able to get an approval for residents to have clothes sent in to them, or to be able to buy them through the inmate store. Eventually 93% of all residents were able to wear their own clothes within the prison.

We were also able to get approval for the men to purchase their own radios. This was a big step back in those days. Probably the biggest victory was to convince the administration to pull the long dividing tables out of the visiting room so that the men could now have contact visits with their families and friends.

"Playboy" and other such magazines and books at that time were also considered contraband. We managed to overcome the censorship policies in this area and now a man could receive literally any type of reading material he was interested in. There were also a lot of small victories connected with the television show and we were feeling pretty high about our successes until the day came when we were to interview the Director of Corrections, Gus Harrison.

Because of the huge number of questions we had received for him we decided to expand the show to an hour. When Harrison arrived he demanded to see the questions in advance of the show. This was something that no other guest was allowed to do so that we could maintain spontaneity and honesty within the program. Peter and I didn't want to let Harrison see the questions, but pressure was applied, and we had no choice but to agree. The director began to throw out half the questions saying that he would not answer them. Benda became incensed over this reaction, since it was understood by the Director that for him to appear on the show he would have to submit to the same formats as all the others' before him. He refused. We cut the show back to half and hour, and upon its completion, Benda handed in a typed three-page resignation to Director Harrison. I hated to see him go and later received a couple of postcards from him out of Canada and Boston.

My next job was as a reporter on the prison newspaper, *"The Spectator"*. Six thousand copies of "The Spectator" were published every Friday and distributed throughout the prison system, the United States and Europe. I worked for "The Spectator" for around six-years. I learned a lot about reporting, writing, and a behind the scenes look at how to get a newspaper printed and published. Within a year I became the editor. During that time I won over 14 personal writing awards and in my last year inside the prison I had brought the paper to national attention by winning the, "National Penal Press Contest," for which I received a beautiful trophy from the University Of Southern Illinois School Of Journalism. I believe we also accomplished a lot through *"The Spectator"*, such as having the censorship of the paper lifted and again promoting many positive changes throughout the prison system.

I also sold many news and special interest articles and photographs to other publications. The local newspaper, *"The Jackson Citizen Patriot"*, reprinted many of my articles, which in-turn was picked up by the wire services. I sold articles and photos to "People Magazine", *The Detroit News"* and "Cat Fancy" magazine, and many other such publications. While working with The Spectator I had my own office to work out of. It consisted of three rooms and my "private" office. It was here that two of my reporters, both from the Tennessee and Kentucky backwoods areas convinced me that they could set up a "still" secretly and we could manufacture at least five gallons of juice (moonshine) each week without the fear of getting caught. So we did and true to their word we were never found out, although we did have a few very close calls. One time in particular was on a weekend when we were all sitting around and watching the Super Bowl on one of the very few TV's in the prison at that time when the Warden walked in to join us. We all had full glasses of "juice" and immediately drank and concealed them until he left. If he ever suspected or knew what we were doing, he never let on or said a thing. At that time, Warden Johnson was a pretty progressive warden and helped us work towards many of the changes that were brought about inside the prison at that time, plus he knew full well that we were all in good standing with the rest of the inmate population and were technically the voice of the inmate. It was also here that I met someone I'll call Mac, who was to become one of my best friends and still is today. Mac is the one who introduced me to LSD and THC and Mescaline and on and on. He is also the one who had most of the outside connections for purchasing and shipping to the prison. He fit right in with our little group and now with us controlling the majority of booze and drugs inside the prison we were all making a substantial amount of money to be sure. I on occasion think back to those days and realize I was making more money in those days than I did in the free world.

After several years and feeling that I had accomplished all I could do with The Spectator I requested a transfer to the photo department. I had always had a fascination with photography and wanted to learn all I could about the subject. I had a good teacher who took me through the steps of how to load and operate a camera and the proper way of taking pictures and finally into the development processes. We worked with both color and black and white photos. It was a relatively young department at the time but prior to that time before I eventually left the photo department we had helped to build it into one of the best photo processing labs in the state. We turned it into a profitable and significant money making business for the institution and gained some degree of a reputation for the quality of work we produced. I especially liked the darkroom work where I'm convinced is the making of a truly good photograph.

While working on *"The Spectator"*, and in the photo department, I also attended classes at Jackson Community College and Wayne State University. For the first time in my life I really got turned on to education and actually enjoyed going to school. There weren't all the outside distractions one encounters when going to school out in the streets, so I was able to concentrate and devote more time to study and reading. I do like to read and there is no better place in the world to wile away the empty hours than to pick up a book and get lost in other worlds. For many years if it was in print, I read it, and went through well over 3,000 books while in prison. I eventually obtained two Associate of Arts Degrees from Jackson Community College and a Bachelors Degree from Wayne State University. I completed a four year college curriculum with a 3.75 GPA, something I would have thought impossible at one time in my life and rather proud of today.

I was also one of the original six men that helped to establish a US Jaycee Chapter inside the prison. It eventually became the largest single organization behind the walls, which provided more services to the inmates than any other program offered by the Corrections Department. They were also one of the consistently top-rated chapters in the state.

Through my position as editor of *"The Spectator"*, and as the institutional photographer, I had free access to all departments and areas of the prison. I also dealt intimately with many of the officials within the prison so I had to be careful about my reputation and the way I carried myself. During all my time in prison I'm proud to say that I never once snitched on or fronted off another inmate even if I considered him an enemy. There were too many better and more effective ways to deal with someone rather than going to an official.

Practically every man that enters prison, sooner or later, gets tested in two areas by his fellow cons. You'll be checked on guts and homosexual tendencies and how you pass these tests will be a big factor in determining how easy or hard your stay in prison will be. Now, the homosexuals in Jackson Prison are quite plentiful and if one leans to that particular persuasion he'll be able to lead a very full and active sex life behind the walls. Although it's not my place to condemn such activities it's just not my cup of tea and I have yet to meet the man that I thought was alluring and attractive. But the day did arrive when I was confronted with such a proposition shortly after my arrival to prison. It happened one day when I was alone with my thoughts in the big yard. Up walked one of the biggest black dudes I'd ever seen. He stood about six-three and must have weighed about 350 pounds. Now, of all the sissies in prison there are some that when they fix themselves up could easily be mistaken for women and found to be attractive by many, but, this big ugly gorilla, who went by the name of Joe Louis, could only be found to be attractive by a tank commander. He was not the most subtle individual in the world and almost immediately started to tell me what he wanted to do to me in the most descriptive terms imaginable, probably hoping that this would turn me on in someway. He then proceeded to tell me that if I would let him do these things to me he would see that I was taken care of and would want for nothing. Now, Joe Louis did have a reputation in prison for being a big, mean, crazy SOB. So, my problem now was, how do you tell a full grown gorilla that could stomp you into the ground with little effort and take what he wanted anyway, that you do not find him or his offer appealing. This became a very tense moment to be sure.

But, very slowly and with extreme care I explained to this man mountain lurching over me that I would not be a good candidate to fill the void in his love life. I think he actually found it hard to believe that I could refuse such a tempting offer and so he upped the ante of goodies he would throw in to sweeten the pot. Again, I told him how flattered I was of his offer, but that I would have to refuse. Luckily the bugle blew, which not unlike the armed services is the prisons way to notify the inmate population that it is time to obey certain rules and activities and this one said it was time to lockup, and so, I was saved from any further conversation with him that day. It took several weeks after that incident of trying to avoid him in the yard, showers and other dark places throughout the prison before he got the hint that I wasn't interested in his propositions. His efforts finally terminated when he damn near terminated me on the football field one day.

Being on rival teams, sometime in the second half of the game, he got the hand-off and was running down the sidelines on my side of the field. So, feeling exceptionally brave, I was going to hit him head-on and finally show him I was not someone to trifle with. Well, unless you've ever tried to stop a locomotive under full steam by throwing your body in front of it you'll never know how hard I was hit. He ran over me like I wasn't even there and proceeded to demolish two more of my teammates on his rush to the goal-line for his touchdown. All three of us spent at least five minutes on our backs in intensive sideline care before we were back on our feet again. I guess that was Joe's way of saying he didn't love me anymore and I was never bothered again by him or any other homosexual since. But, that ended the old axiom for me that "sissies" are not necessarily "sissies".

I did develop a few intimate friendships with some of the men in prison, who to this day, I consider the best, most sincere, trusting friends I have in this world. Unfortunately they are all in for murder charges and all serving life sentences. These men are also considered by many within the prison system to be the most dangerous, fearsome and untrustworthy around. But, if we will look past the crime and look into the person himself you just may be surprised to find great compassion, intelligence, respect, love and worth. No matter whatever happens, these are men I can always trust and depend upon.

These are the men that I ran with daily while in prison. Back in the '60s and early '70s, things in prison were much different than they are today. There was a different type of inmate. There weren't as many prisons in the state and a man was respected for the way he carried himself and who he ran with. For a time; about two years, our little group literally ran the prison. We controlled the majority of the gambling, drugs, booze, protection and policies within the prison. It was almost a good and bearable life behind those huge cement walls for a few years. There was plenty of money, drugs and other little luxuries to help make life more bearable. It was a time when I experimented heavily with drugs. I smoked marijuana to dropping acid and LSD, heroin, speed and drank a lot of spud juice. I tried it all and tried to lose myself as often as possible.

For two years in *"The Spectator"*, as I had stated earlier I had a couple of southerners working for me and every week they would setup 25 gallons of juice, (moonshine) and on Fridays we would strain it and sell whatever we didn't drink to other thirsty inmates.

Probably some of the most memorable experiences I had while in prison were spent with a good friend and co-worker in the photo department. Mac, as he liked to be called, was about six-two at about 220 pounds. Now those figures are a bit deceptive without seeing him. Mac was all muscle and hard as a rock with a reputation of being one tough son-of-a-bitch. Convicted of killing one man, and suspected of several others Mac is presently serving a life sentence courtesy of the State of Michigan.

Mac and I lived pretty well for a couple of years inside the walls of Jackson Prison. We spent most of our time in those few years together in the basement of the prison auditorium. There, we had our own large private office, photo lab, and darkroom setup. As the institutional photographers we had work details that allowed us to remain out of our cells from 6:00 o'clock AM to 10:00 o'clock PM everyday, seven days a week, with free access to anyplace and department within the prison confines. We found that so long as we had a camera in our hands, or looped over a shoulder, we exhibited a certain degree of importance and no official ever questioned our movements. If one did, we would quickly complain to a superior that we were being hampered or harassed in performing our duties, whether it was true or not. Such maneuvers soon spread throughout the officer ranks and we were never troubled again.

Although Mac is not the one who formally introduced me to the drug scene he sure helped in furthering my education in this area. It wasn't long before Mac and I literally controlled the majority of sales and distribution of drugs within the prison. One hit of acid, that we would pay anywhere from fifty to seventy-five cents for, would sell inside the prison for five dollars or more for a hit. Needless to say this provided a good return on one's initial investment. So, it wasn't long before we were living like little sheiks in exile. Plus, besides the drug trade we also controlled the photography concession which provided us with another big buck income behind the walls. Everyone it seemed wanted a photo of themselves and friends to either send home to a loved one or to keep in the memory department.

Like I said, we had our own private office which in itself was somewhat of a status symbol but it was soon to become much more than just an office. For about two weeks we went on a scavenger hunt for things we could put to use in the office. Things like two nice leather easy chairs, courtesy of the upholstery shop. A couch that we confiscated from the psych clinic, a deep pile wall to wall carpet from the Academic school along with a set of draperies to keep prying eyes out. After all, we were a photo department and we had to maintain a certain form of darkness for our light sensitive equipment. A few large cushions from the Top-6 area, a Heath kit component system with five well placed speakers and a television set from the radio shop and Vocational school. Then it was a few gallons of very expensive paint from the paint shop, five large colored strobe lights from the stage of the auditorium, a small gallery of original oil paintings and photo art, and approximately 350 pounds of weights to keep fit with. On the back wall we painted a huge mural of a Chinese dragon spitting fire. A true junkie's paradise to be sure that would rival most interior designs in "Home Beautiful" magazine. Many a day I spent on the floor cushions totally blasted out of my mind listening to the reverberations of Pink Floyd pounding out of the five stereo speaker hookups. That room was a beautiful escape plan and was successful enough to allow Mac and me to successfully cheat the state out of more than two years of our time. I actually enjoyed myself and hated to leave the place when the time came. One reason we got away so long with living like that is because it was probably the only place in the entire prison that a guard was not allowed to go without permission. We were able to keep the door locked at all times with a sign posted on it's front stating that it could not be shaken down or searched without first getting permission from the warden. The reason of course was because of all the light sensitive materials stored in the photo lab. The way that little sign came about is because on one shakedown the (screws) officers actually did open up boxes of paper and film looking for contraband. Of course when the light touched it, it was ruined. When we found out that they had opened a few boxes we naturally opened a few more after they left to the tune of about $5,000.00 worth of damage. When the state got the bill, the next day the sign went up. So, in that sense we had it made.

On the few occasions when we had to actually handle our own drugs, what better place to carry it than in the back of a camera. "Hey, officer, don't touch that camera, ya wanna expose the film?" So, we almost became untouchable within the prison confines. Why we were never caught in such often states of drugged mindlessness I'll never know because we sure gave them plenty of chances. I remember that for three years in a row we had to photograph the nurses graduation ceremonies held in the officer's dining room. Besides the five or six inmate grads, there would be three or four doctors, a couple of registered nurses, the warden and his two deputies, along with a scattering of other prison officials. The first of these photo sessions is the most memorable as that is when I was breaking Mac in on the proper use of the camera. It just so happened that prior to this assignment we had both dropped a hit of acid figuring we were through for the day when the call came over the phone that we had to report to the OD, "Officers Dinning" to photograph the ceremony. So, grabbing up our cameras we were off on our first adventure together. Of course, when we got there we just knew that every doctor and nurse could tell what condition we were in but, since we had little choice in the matter, we decided to play it through as well as possible.

A dinner was served first and trying to be as inconspicuous as possible we picked a seat at the end of the table and tried to stay out of any conversations. That, of course, didn't work and what we must have sounded like in our destroyed state of mind must have been something for posterity. Especially as I and other participants watched Mac scraping his peas off his lap and me trying to maintain some form of controlled sophistication.

When it came time to work, I started to slowly walk around the room clicking my camera at anything that moved. When I had worked my way behind the speakers table I noticed everyone in the room staring toward the corner at the back of the room. Looking through my viewfinder I soon found out what everyone was looking at. There was poor Mac sitting in a chair with the back open on the camera and film trailing out of it looped around his neck and arms and falling to the floor. He had a strange resemblance to a scientific ape searching through the rabble of film for some hidden treasure. Quickly I worked my way over to him and tried to position myself between him and his adoring audience asking, "What's the matter?" Still pulling film out of the back of the camera he calmly informed me that he was having a seizure of insanity and I'd better do something quick. First off I noticed that he hadn't opened the back of the camera in the conventional way. Instead, with his brute strength he had torn it open and folded it back. So, I told him to put the film back in the camera, which he did, by wadded handfuls and pressing the back, back down on it, we nonchalantly backed out the door clicking our cameras like we knew what we were doing.

For nearly two years thereafter we got caught in such states of mind when filming the nurses' graduation but fortunately were able to compose ourselves enough during those ceremonies that no repercussions were ever experienced.

Another incident that happened in the Officers Dining (OD) room took place one day when Mac handed me what he thought was 10 hits of THC. With our drug resistances built up at this point in time we split the package and each dropped five hits apiece. Well, it didn't take more than a half an hour to figure out that what we took was not THC. As we quietly stared at each other and watched the sweat begin to gather on our foreheads I cleverly said, "I don't think this stuff is THC, Mac." "I know," he answered. "We're gonna die, aren't we?", "Yup!" he answered. So, we figured if we had to go we may as well go out in style. And what better way to go than with a good meal and a good fight. The only place to get a good meal was in the OD. And the only people we were interested in fighting were the guards. So, off we went. We got through the security gates with our passes, went up the stairs, and grabbing a plate, fell right into line with the rest of the officers not one of which questioned our presence there. Upon heaping our plates with all the delicacies not served to the rest of the cons we entered the dining room, had a seat, and began to enjoy ourselves. Finally, figuring out that we were on some kind of weird acid trip we began to laugh ourselves silly, food spraying disgustingly out of our mouths and rolling down our chins, and ultimately reverting back to our prehistoric ancestry as we began feeding ourselves with our bare hands and letting it squish between our fingers.

Now, all this time the guards, about 15 of them, just stared at us and said nothing. It was unbelievable. Any other time we would have been swarmed over and hauled off to the hole. But for some unexplained reason, they did not react this time. They just sat there and watched us make fools of ourselves probably thinking we knew something they didn't. Otherwise, why would these two nuts have the guts to be doing what they were doing? Well, sometime during that feast we started to peak and knew we hadn't overdosed and that we weren't going to die. So, finishing up, we quietly slinked out of the OD and back to the "Dragon's Den", which we appropriately named our little hide-a-way, and damn near laughed ourselves to death.

Some other little games that Mac and I used to engage in when under the influence of some form of drug was to walk up on a group of harmonizing blacks and join in singing our rendition of "On the Wings of a Snow White Dove", which of course would illicit incredulous stares in our direction wondering who these crazy honkies were. But, like I said earlier, Mac was so damn big and bad no one really wanted to hassle him so we got away with a lot of stuff most inmates couldn't have.

A few times we would freak out guys in the mess hall when we would reach across the table to each other's plates and grab a handful of mashed potatoes or corn, or if I thought his piece of meat looked better than mine then I would snatch it and eat it. Most guys just tried not to notice us, but others, not knowing that we were friends would sit back wide-eyed and wait for the small riot that they knew for sure was to ensue.

Once, while standing on the crowded ramp entrance to the dining hall Mac spotted a Mexican (Chicano) who owed us some money and shouting out to cover his back he bullied his way through a mass of humanity to confront him. As I watched, Mac bunched up the front of the Mexican's shirt and pushed him up against a railing. I took my position at his back and turned around to face off any opposition that might try to interfere and damn near soiled myself when I saw what was pushing its way through the crowd heading straight toward us. There must have been at least 20 more Chicano's coming right at us. Mac in the meantime was gently roughing up his prey trying to put the fear of God into him. "Ah, Mac!" I said, trying to get his attention. "Ah, Mac, I think there is something you ought to know", I said quietly tugging at his sleeve. But Mac just ignored me and continued to illicit the right answers from his victim. Well, I just knew we were dead as I knew everyone of the 20 Chicano's heading our way was strapped down with a knife or shiv of some kind. So, now all that was left for me to do was to face them off with the hope that they didn't see the panic and tears welling up in my eyes. I figured I might get at least one punch in before I looked like one of mom's pin cushions. Well never let it be said that I wasn't lucky at least one time in my life. It just so happened that the little Chicano fellow that Mac was pressing was an outcast and equally disliked by his fellow Latin Americans. The leader of the approaching band looked at me and said, "Go ahead and tell Mac to do what he wants with him. We'll make sure no one interferes".

"Ah, yeah! Right!" I answered intelligently, trying not to let my sigh of relief carry into the next county. But, as it happened, a few pushes and shoves and by lifting the guy up on his tip-toes by way of Mac's hand around his throat he got the message and the confrontation ended peacefully.

Another time Mac and I had an unwanted co-worker assigned to the photo department which of course was not something we accepted well considering all the various activities we were involved in and who it was apparent was trying to ingratiate himself with our superiors. It came to a point where he was actually starting to snitch on us. Luckily we had a great supervisor who took it all with a grain of salt and paid the informant little or no mind. But with such a diversification of activities that we were involved in we couldn't take the chance that he would find another ear to bend. If we took him out completely it might screw up a few things for us so we decided to drop a couple boxes of squares (cigarettes) on a couple of brothers and pointed the target out. The next day as our problem left the photo lab he was way-laid quite effectively with the message that he'd better lock himself up, or seek a transfer, because Jackson just became too small for them all to live in together.

Well, apparently one of their blows must have hit him too hard on the head because the next day the damn fool actually confronted our supervisor and pointed his finger at me and said that I was probably the one who arranged the beating. Immediately seeing my eyes light up at that statement our supervisor said he didn't have time to discuss it right now and had an important meeting he had to attend to right away and left. Now I was alone with the snitch. He looked at me and I grinned back at him. Leaping up he broke for the door at a dead run with me right on his heels. I chased him out of the auditorium, around through the sub-hall and into a counselor's office where he thought he could find some refuge and protection. But it just so happened he chose <u>my</u> counselor's office to seek help. Seeing the fire in my eyes the counselor stepped out of his office mumbling something about having to go to the bathroom. I slammed the snitch up against the wall and started to strangle him when about five of my good friends from *"The Spectator"* office which was located just across the hallway burst into the office and pulled me off him. They escorted me back to the office to calm down a bit. But what was interesting is that two of these friends stayed behind and finished the job for me which resulted in the snitch being transferred outside to the Trusty Division the next week. And to this day neither my counselor nor supervisor has ever said a thing about it.

Besides all our other extra-curricular activities Mac and I would test out various escape plans from this Southern Michigan paradise. But the closest we ever came to actually executing one is from an article we found once in a "Mechanics Illustrated" magazine that showed how to build your own two-man helicopter. So off we went on another scavenger hunt. We actually got just about everything we needed together. The frame was built in the Maintenance and Welding shops, the wheels from somewhere else, and a motor from an old gas operated washing machine. The only thing we couldn't put together was the large overhead propeller, and most important, where to store it until we were ready to fly it out of there. But I like to think we came close to it and if we could have found a way to make the propeller they'd still be looking for us.

But, all good things must come to an end, and one evening while Mac and I were in the middle of deep-fat-frying a couple of chickens in our darkroom kitchen all hell broke loose. Being too secure in our surroundings we forgot that it was movie night for the rest of the population and that the mouth watering aroma of Kentucky Fried Chicken was wafting up through the floor and throughout the entire auditorium. As luck would have it a new sergeant just transferred inside from another institution, which either couldn't read or just didn't believe in signs that said he couldn't enter - entered. There we were in our plush little nether world half sitting and laying on the carpet with the stereo going full blast. There we were with a chicken leg in each hand and grease dribbling down our chins. "What the hell is going on down here?" he shouted. "What do you think you're doing? Where do you assholes think you are?"

Well I'm sorry to say, I didn't have any quick or clever answers to those questions, and that turned out to be our last night in the Dragons Den. When the officials and administration saw the way the place was laid out they just couldn't believe that such a place could exist inside the prison. For the next two weeks thereafter it became a show place for every official in the prison system to see. When everyone was made aware of its existence they proceeded to lock the place down and for two weeks, day and night, they shook the place down, tearing out ceilings and walls looking for our stash of goodies.

Mac and I just knew we would be spending the next three years in the hole. As it was, about six tickets (disciplinary reports) were written on us, but somehow we managed to beat them all, with the exception of having contraband chicken in our possession. For that offense we drew a couple of days in the hole. When we were released and told to remove our personal property from the photo lab we found that in all the places they tore apart and looked they still missed our stash (the money and drugs). Unbelievable! So, as Mac held their attention I discretely removed it and off we went to our new office, courtesy of the administration. Within two weeks we had that office redecorated to rival the old one and we were back in business again. In fact it became much easier for the staff and officers that had been bribed to reach us and deliver any merchandise we placed an order for.

Now, I know, one of the big questions in and out of prison is how do inmates get their drugs, money, etc. Sure, the obvious is to bribe an officer or official. Of course that happens, but when a bust comes down it's just not worth it. Yes, we always had a couple on the payroll but our main supply and quantity came from much easier and safer sources. In the days of blotter acid we received deliveries almost on a daily basis. How? Our outside connection would drop a hit on a piece of construction paper, the kind that grade school kids use in art classes. Such paper came in all different colors. When it dried they would draw kid pictures on them, stick figures, hearts and flowers with messages such as "Happy Birthday Dad" or "Miss You Uncle", etc. Then when we received them delivered directly to our cells at mail call we would hold them up to the light and grid the drop spots out. There would be approximately 50 to 60 hits to a sheet of paper that we paid 75 cents for and sold for five bucks or more a hit. The guards and censors thought it sweet that we stayed in contact with our little ones.

Books were always being donated to the prison and of course the prison encourages such donations. So did we, and in pill form, mescaline, acid and the small stuff came with such book donations. When a box of books arrived the guards would pull them all out and go through them checking every page and even the spines to make sure there was no contraband hidden within them. Once satisfied, they would put the books back in the box and give them to us to distribute.

Ever hear the story of the guy who stole wheel barrels? Every night he would pass through a guard station where they would inspect his wheel barrel for contraband. After several months the head guard asked what he was doing. "I know you're stealing something, and since you'll no longer be here, could you tell me what it was you were stealing?" "Sure", said the man, "wheel barrels".

Once back in our office we emptied the books out and cut open the boxes. Remember what a card board box looks like? The walls or corrugated sides of a box are perfect for stuffing hundreds of small pills down into. Thus, the box itself becomes our wheel barrel. For the larger stuff like pot, marijuana, knives and guns, yup, six small automatics came inside the prison this way, and yes, they were eventually all found, I think - were stuffed inside fire extinguishers.

Every few months all the extinguishers throughout the prison had to be inspected along with the running of fire drills. Jackson Prison had its own inmate Volunteer Fire Department; it was based just outside the walls within the Trusty Division. The fire chief, a friend of ours from inside the walls for many years prior to being released to TD was very helpful in securing our treasures in selected extinguishers. Jackson Prison, a self sustaining prison system, had several prison farms around its walls raising everything from cattle, pigs, chickens and vegetables. There were no fences or guard towers around the farms thus it was easy for nightly drop-offs to be made at designated spots along the desolated country roads to be picked up the next day and passed along to the fire inspector. And that's just a few of the ways we acquired what necessities we needed inside the impenetrable walls of Jackson Prison.

But unfortunately the wheels were in motion to split Mac and me up and within a few months I was transferred to the Trusty Division, and several months after that Mac got himself busted with a significant cache of drugs, weapons and money that someone snitched out. What was cute about that bust is that the warden snitched out the snitch to us, and when they sent him outside to Trusty Division, little did he know that we had arranged a nice little reception for him.

Putting him on call to the basement gym in 16 Block at a time when it would be completely empty with the exception of four of us waiting for him. He gingerly walked into the trap. Unfortunately one of the guys revealed him self too soon and sensing the danger the snitch broke and ran before we could get to him. We lost our chance that time but we saw to it that the word was spread throughout the prison that he was poison and for the rest of his stay in Jacktown he was constantly watching his back and totally cut-off and ostracized by the rest of the inmate population. He paid a little for his indiscretion but not as much as Mac who was transferred north to Marquette Prison which is Michigan's ultimate security facility. The next I heard from him was through the grapevine and a newspaper article that said he was caught trying to tunnel out with a few other guys. Bless his heart, he never gives up.

In the years that I was at Jackson there were a couple of tense moments that could have erupted into riots. Once was when there was a power failure and all the lights went out. The only people who really panicked were the guards who all ran for the Control Center and left the entire prison virtually unguarded from about 8:30 pm until 2:00 am. All the prisoners roamed about leisurely with sticks and ball bats breaking things and scaring people. Myself and a couple of friends went to the security of the Civil Defense office and with hardhats, flashlights and pipes locked ourselves in and woe to anyone who attempted to break in there. But fortunately the weather was stormy, wet and windy so most of the men eventually locked themselves back up. I don't think anyone even tried to escape.

Another time was during a strike of the Industries department that soon spread throughout the system. Everyone demanded a raise in pay up to a dollar a day. Inmates in Jackson Prison were responsible for the making and production of all the license plates in the state along with all street and highway signs in the state. All the hospital sheets, gowns and uniforms were also made there along with the majority of paper forms in use throughout the state. Now, the Director of Corrections had just appointed Perry Johnson to be the new warden following the retirement of George Kropp. After about the forth day of the strike when virtually the entire prison was at a standstill he approached me with his Deputy Warden, Charles Egeler, and asked what he could do to end the strike. He had called Governor Milliken for advice on how to handle the situation but the governor told Johnson, "That was why he had the job". So, I suggested to him what I would do and say to the population. Simply, that he get on the institutional phone hook up and talk to the men like adults with respect and no threats and tell them, "there was nothing he could do, as the warden, towards getting them a dollar a day raise in pay. That such action had to come through the legislature". If he was in sympathy of our cause, as he said he was, he would promise to continue in his efforts to get us a raise. That night he did just that and the next day the strike was broken without threats reprisals or violence.

All my life I had been athletically inclined towards most all sports. I loved them all and loved to participate in whatever game came my way. In prison I was no different and I was always on a football, softball or tennis team. I played a lot of handball and at one time or another won every tournament held at the prison, or was on the winning team. No doubt, the best way to let off steam in prison is on the football field. There you can get rid of your aggressions and it's legal. I'd been on a football team every year in prison and win or loose I loved the game and did in fact get rid of a lot of my aggressions.

The most violent and successful year we had on the football field was 1972. I was on an all white team called the "Vikings", consisting primarily of lifers and murderers. Practically every team we played against was all black. Although I don't think it started out that way, it seemed that every battle on the field turned into small race wars. We were the team to beat. In just one season alone I had my nose broken at least twice and took nine stitches at the side of my right eye.

We had a big 285 pound center that once played for Michigan State University. In his second game he had his entire jaw blown out along with all his teeth; uppers and lowers, and he was out for the season. Two men on the team left because of broken legs and one more with a broken arm. Of course there were always the assorted cuts, bruises and contusions. In fact, in one of our final games one of our team-mates was actually killed when he was hit just right in the chest as he was attempting to catch a pass. And that was just the injuries on our team. Believe me; we inflicted just as heavy casualties on the opposing team members. We went undefeated that year winning 36 straight games. In a play off game one of the opposing players actually pulled a knife and began to slash it around because he thought someone had hit him too hard. In the final championship game they virtually locked up the entire prison on a Saturday morning and the game was broadcast over the prison closed circuit radio system. They stationed guards on the roofs with rifles, put two rolling stretchers on the side lines with a couple of inmate nurses and told us to go at it. We played an all-black team called the "Black Disciples". It was a war to remember. The entire prison; guards and inmates alike were betting on this game and waited for the outcome. I think we only won by one touchdown but we did win, and only suffered a few casualties.

That was the last year for full contact football without the benefit of pads or protection. From that point on, the administration required all football teams to be integrated, referees would be schooled, and flag football would be the only type of game played and a whole new set of rules were installed. But it was fun while it lasted.

Believe it or not a death or murder in prison is just as frightening and scary an experience as those that take place in a free society. Imagine, if you can, a community of about 5,000 people that have an annual murder rate of approximately three to seven each and every year. This is a closed community that sees approximately 50 to 100 stabbings, rapes and violent attacks every year. In just three short summer months in 1980 there were 22 serious stabbings that took place inside the walls.

In the years that I've spent there I've seen or been witness to several such attacks and deaths. I've seen a few men stabbed repeatedly in the prison yard and dining hall and attempt to hold their intestines in while staggering to the infirmary for help. I've seen a man strike fear in an entire auditorium full of men as he ran through it, down the aisles and over the backs of seats swinging a huge homemade machete while in pursuit of another inmate he was trying to chase down. I've seen men both fall and be pushed off the fourth gallery; four stories high, landing to an inevitable death with shattering thuds on the hard terrazzo floors below. Probably the most fearful death in prison is being burned alive in your locked cell. Once the victim's cell door is shut; the tip of a pencil is broken off in the door lock preventing it from being opened by a guard with a key. Then, another inmate passes by with a coffee jar full of naphtha or gasoline that is shattered inside the cell with the helpless victim locked in, and then followed by a lit match. In a six by eight foot cell there is nowhere to hide and no way to extinguish the flames as they eat hungrily at his flesh. The horrible screams and pleas for help are impossible to ignore and remain a part of one's dreams for a lifetime.

A definite understatement, prison is not a nice place to live. Sure, there are amusing and light moments that occur from time to time, but unless one is able to align himself with one of the stronger or ruling cliques in prison it becomes a frightening and terrifying experience to be sure.

Some of the more humorous and lighter moments I can remember while in prison involve the great helicopter escape; when the friend's of Dale Remling high-jacked a small helicopter and had the pilot slip over the back wall to land in an open area near the old cannery building and take off again with Remling aboard. The guards and administration officials all stood around scratching their heads and other parts of their anatomies, wondering what had just happened. One thing that never ceases to amaze me is that when an escape does happen, especially one of this caliber, the escapee always either goes home or to a place that they are known. In this case, Remling goes to his old bar for a drink. The news of this incredible escape is wide spread, and of course someone notices him and a phone call is made to the authorities and he is quickly sent home to prison. Stupid.

One time while trying to establish some control over the rising pigeon population behind the walls several guards took to the roofs with their shotguns and then when they scared the birds into the air they cut loose. On this particular day there must have been at least five guards on the roof and when the pigeons took wing the guards raised their guns and fired a resounding volley of shots into the middle of the swarm. But, I think the combined laughter of the hundreds of inmates watching from below in the yard was just as deafening as the shotgun fire. As when the firing stopped it was only one lonely pin-feather that fell to the ground out of that huge flock of pigeons. It floated delicately back to earth into the crowd of laughing spectators. I'm sure that after such a wonderful display of marksmanship a hundred new escape plans were formulating in the minds below.

Then there was the time we had a pigs vs. freaks football game. Our varsity football team played the men of the Detroit Police Department. At that time I was the institutional photographer and responsible for recording the game for posterity on film. Everyone in prison was excited that day whether they played or not. It was a chance to let off some steam and get in a few licks towards some of the people who had helped put them there. Prior to the game I was besieged by our players to make sure that I positioned myself properly so that I could get a picture of them hitting a cop, since now, it would be legal. I don't think any of our team cared whether we won the game or not so long as they won the fight.

Well, when the game took place it turned into what everyone figured it would be. It turned into an organized free-for-all on the football field. I took several pictures of cops and cons being carried off the field on stretchers. I complied with requests of, "Here, get this one Herr", as a con drew back and slugged or elbowed one of Detroit's finest. Once when I missed a shot of a friend named Virgil decking an officer in the end-zone he actually called the play a second time so I'd have a second shot. Another shot consisted of a huge black dude named Eddy D., who slammed the ball carrier to the ground at my feet, and looking up, to make sure I was ready, pulled the cops helmet up and planted a great big wet kiss on his lips. I don't even remember who eventually won the game, or the fight, for that matter, but needless to say we never had another pigs vs. freaks game in the institution again.

Of course some of you I'm sure have heard of Ron LeFlore, who the Detroit Tigers drafted out of prison and still may hold the team's all-time bases stolen record. Besides being a good baseball and softball player, LeFlore also used to play a lot of football in the fall and winter months around the prison. Make no mistake about it, he was fast, and damn near impossible to catch once he got the ball and a little bit of running room. So, anytime he played end or wide receiver it was Mac's and my job to double team him and make sure he never got off or across the line of scrimmage. Actually, we were quite successful at this endeavor and maneuver. Mac would hit him high and I would hit him low and lay on him until the play was in progress. LeFlore would switch back and forth from one end of the scrimmage line to the other trying to get away from us but we just switched with him. I know we must have driven him crazy every time his team played against us but our strategy always worked much to his displeasure and anger when we hit him a little too hard sometimes.

Another name of some renown that I was privileged to meet while I was in prison, was that of Lonnie Chambers, aka "Little Beaver". Now, I don't expect too many kids today to relate to that name, but many years ago, Little Beaver was the Indian side-kick to cowboy star Red Ryder. Depicted in cartoons, movies and comic books, Chambers was one of the first men to play the roll of Little Beaver. Sentenced to life in prison for murder, Little Beaver did indeed serve out his sentence to the very end, broke, lonely and forgotten. At one time a friend and I attempted to gather information on Little Beaver for a book we were going to write about him. But from inside a prison cell we found the going to be tough in gathering what information we needed. The motion picture studios we wrote to never answered us and the prison officials we got to pull his records were amazed at how skimpy his files were. There were discrepancies on when he originally came to prison. There was no date of birth on record for him and hardly any information at all on the crime itself. A full blooded American Indian, who had spent the past 20-plus years in prison, Little Beaver reminisced with us prior to his death. He told us about the shows and movies he appeared in which also included Buffalo Bills Wild West Show. He told us about the audiences before the Kings and Queens of England and Spain, and his meetings with several presidents of the United States. He shared stories from when he had his trading post in Northern Michigan and the proud pictures he shared of himself mounted on his horse in full Indian dress. He actually was a chief, yet this proud man, who helped to bring joy and entertainment to so many lives in the early 1920s, '30s and '40s, was allowed to die lonely and forgotten in a stinking prison hole. What a poor commentary on our times and society.

While editor of the prison newspaper I was also instrumental in arranging a few rock concerts to be held behind the walls. Working with the editor of "Crème" magazine, Barry Kramer, we were able to book groups such as, "The Savage Grace, Mitch Ryder and The Detroit Wheels, The Third Power and The Wilson Mower Pursuit". But, long hair and loud music didn't set well with the present ruling administration. So, such future rock concerts were eventually cancelled by order of Director Perry Johnson.

My artistic endeavors also progressed at this time of my life. Every Sunday night prior to the time of television and radios being allowed in prison, we had a radio earphone hookup in each cell. The favorite program of the residents was the "Lou Gordon Show". He was a very outspoken journalist, television commentator and interviewer. Lou was the Bill O'Rielly of his time so to speak. Although many of us didn't agree with a lot of his views he did represent the feelings of a vast majority of citizens in the free world.

At any rate, I saw an article and picture of him in a recent "Time" magazine and decided to do his portrait. It turned out pretty well, so

I sent it to him. What was to follow next was totally unexpected. He showed the portrait on his television program and carried on about it so much you would have thought I was the next Rembrandt. He wrote me back asking, "If there were any art supplies that I needed?" Going through art catalogues I made an extensive list of a number of items I could use stating that any one item would be greatly appreciated. A couple of weeks later I was called over to the Hobby Craft department of the prison and asked to sign for a box of supplies. The box stood as high as I did, about two feet square and contained every single item on the list I had sent to Gordon. Unbelievable.

Well, if it worked once I thought, it ought to work again, right? I looked for pictures and portraits to draw. Stan and Isadore Winkleman, of the Winkleman womens clothing chain were next. They were so happy with their portraits that they invited my wife Pauline to one of their stores where she received the red carpet treatment along with a shopping spree courtesy of the house of Winkleman. She was told to take whatever she wanted.

Then there was philanthropist, Max Fisher, who sent me a nice check for pictures that I donated to his New Detroit project. There was a portrait of J.P. McCarthy and his new wife of WJR Radio fame followed by a check from Richard Harvill, then the President of Arizona State University. There were numerous flattering and complementary letters from Governors Romney and Milliken, as well as US Senators; Philip Hart and Robert Griffin. American Ambassador to the Philippines and future Michigan Supreme Court Justice, G. Mennon Williams, movie and television actresses; Kathy Garver and Deborah Walley were also to join my gallery of portraits. Requests were now pouring in to me for paintings. I didn't have to seek the work out any longer as it came to me. There were special jobs done for the Warden and Director of Corrections, State Senator Smeekens, the Holiday Inn in Ft. Wayne, Indiana as well as inmates, art shows, friends and relatives. I painted for almost two years exclusively for various mafia families. I was always busy and couldn't keep up with the work but enjoyed it greatly. Another of my secret desires is to be able to do nothing but paint and draw, preferably in the Philippines and of the people of that country who I truly feel a kinship with.

Probably one of the nicest, most honest and sincerest persons that I've ever met in my life was Alexis Praus. At that time Praus was the

Director of the Kalamazoo Public Museum. He saw my artwork and took me under his wing. He helped promote my work, and not only in the State of Michigan where he arranged for my work to be shown; in several one man shows, and art stores, but helped to sell it and take orders as he traveled around the world to various countries in his position as a curator with the museum.

There were many newspaper articles and features on me about my art at this time of my life. I painted under the name of DiPaul because everything I did was partly inspired by my wife, Pauline. So, I combined our names, Dick and Pauline, thus DiPaul. A good majority of my work was given to Pauline who either sold it or gave it away. I wish I knew the whereabouts of a lot of that which I sent to her. Some of it I was very proud of and wish she would have kept it. I believe the media for which I excelled in the most was charcoal and pastels but was also beginning to make some strides in oil.

During those first long years in prison I fell more and more in love with Pauline. She was doing everything she could for me. Writing letters, meeting people and working hard to get me out of there. I received a letter from her every single day for over six years. Through those letters and frequent visits to see me we came to know each other much better and I was so much in love with her it hurt. But, I was in prison and not home with her where I belonged. The tremendous disappointments she received from the attorneys we had hired, the pressures of raising a family alone, the financial burdens mounting and the needs of a woman for companionship with a man were too much for her to bear. Pauline began to date other men. Although I'm certainly in no position to characterize and judge others I don't think she used her head too well when she began to enter the dating scene once again. The horror stories I received from my children and even from her at that time did nothing for my piece of mind behind the walls. She would promise to break off the relationships, did, and then ultimately be back with some jerk over and over again and again. For over a year I feared for my children's and her safety and there was literally nothing that I could do about it.

Then there came a time when for over a month I received no mail and couldn't reach anyone by phone. Her mother eventually admitted to having the kids but said, "She had no idea where Pauline was." I was frantic with worry. Then one day I was called out for a visit. It was Pauline, and she looked like death warmed over. She admitted to having gone off with some guy for a few weeks, but the straw that broke the proverbial camels back was when this day, she brought her jocker to the prison with her. There he sat, only a few chairs away visiting another inmate. I couldn't believe she would do this to me. I almost went insane. I wanted to kill them both right then and there. Imagine sitting in the same room with my wife and her lover, and him grinning back at me, knowing there was nothing I could do about it. No way would I remain there any longer. I got up and walked over to him, my head buzzing, my heart beating rapidly and my mind reeling with murderous thoughts. I was going to kill him right then and there. Pauline ran after me trying to pull me back from him. When I finally reached him, would you believe the damn fool just grinned up at me and offered me a seat? I told him where he could put his seat and how I was going to suck the breath out of his heart when a couple of friends in the visiting room saw what was going down and helped to restrain me and get me out of there.

That was the day I fell out of love and would never have anything to do with Pauline again. It's only been recently that I've been able to forgive her for that little indiscretion. Nothing had ever hurt me more in life. I felt betrayed and humiliated and have been trying to understand what happened. It was a time of great emotional instability for me and I almost did something very foolish. Something like putting out a contract on both Pauline and her lover. One of my good friends at the time was soon to be released on parole and volunteered to take care of the situation for me if I so desired. Less than six months after that incident a large grave was dug in Haslett, Michigan and several bags of lye were lying beside the hole. All that was needed was my final okay to give over the phone and the deed would have been done.

But, I couldn't do it. I could not throw the years we did have together away. I could not subject my kids to that type of life. One parent was already taken from them and no matter how much I hated Pauline for what she had done I couldn't' cheat them out of another parent. So, reluctantly I cancelled the contract over the phone. One week later the person who was to fulfill my contract was arrested for another contract murder he performed successfully in Detroit and was sentenced to a life term back at Jackson Prison. He eventually did serve out that sentence when he died behind the walls. But it was that incident that prompted me to file for a divorce which was ultimately granted and separating us from each other forever.

The next few years were emotionally hard times for me. I was not allowed to see the kids anymore and it was sometime before Pauline even wrote me again to let me know how they were doing, although I had employed an attorney to seek help from the courts for an order to let me see them again. Eventually we were successful in arranging a visit when I was in the prison camp system. But that only lasted one time until there was supposedly an anonymous phone call to the State Police indicating that I was planning to escape. That little maneuver by someone was enough to have me thrown back in prison and canceling any further visits I might have with my children. Eventually such an escape plan was proven to be false and the "anonymous" phone caller never identified. But his or "her" dirty work had been done.

As I've said, it was a period of loneliness and depression. About the only visitor I had was Linda Powell. She was a kind of shirt-tail cousin. She and I grew up together with her grandfather, Earl Blair who married my grandmother Marion. Pauline and Linda never really got along together which is something I never understood as Linda was a good friend to me, and nothing more, although I'm afraid Pauline thought otherwise. So, there came a time when Linda introduced me to a friend and business associate of hers named, Bette. I needed someone to talk to and visit with besides another inmate. Bette helped to fill that void.

Over the next several years our relationship grew and developed into daily letters and frequent visits. I found Bette very attractive, intelligent and fun to be with. I think she literally saved my life at that period of time. I also think Bette had as many emotional problems and hang-ups as I did. But together we were able to talk and sort things out. We began to make plans for the future and contrary to what some people may claim; I feel it was through Bette's dedicated efforts that I was eventually paroled.

During these few years of visits and correspondence we grew closer and closer together and I eventually asked her to marry me. She was everything I dreamed of and a way I thought, of putting my life back together again. Through money that I had managed to save we invested in a business called, "Castle Island". It was a janitorial service and together we managed to build it into something we were proud of.

From inside the prison I devised ads and logos and put together various work sheets. We employed up to seven people at one time and it looked like all was going great. As I had referred to earlier I was making a lot of money in prison, through selling drugs and booze and photos and protection and gambling, and my paintings. Probably thirty percent of the time I was paid off in cigarettes and other goods but the other seventy percent was in good old hard cash that I passed along through the visiting rooms and outgoing mail. Of course all incoming mail was opened and censored prior to being delivered to the inmate. But outgoing mail is never opened. Thus, I just slipped a couple of 100 dollar bills at a time in my letters to my sister. Bette and Linda. All opened separate bank accounts that I could periodically withdraw from to buy bedroom furniture and clothes and dance classes for my children and to help support Bette and a friend of hers in their efforts to open a new business. Bette helped to retain the services of Brisbois and Sturtz, attorneys out of Saginaw to help get me out of there. Through their combined efforts, Bette's letters to various officials and even her visits to the Parole Board on my behalf all helped to secure my parole. But it was also learned and intimated via the Parole Board that I would be looked upon more favorably if I was married. So, over the next few months I designed a ring representing my feelings for her and asked Bette to marry me. I don't believe that either one of us wanted to get married right then, especially with my being in prison. But, the past years and the pressures of the system dictated differently. Throughout my years there I've seen the Parole Board "unofficially", force men and women into unwanted marriages before they would be granted a parole. As though inmates who got married would look better on their records, justifying to themselves that a man had supposedly settled down and would start a family. I think the statistics will show that marriages that take place inside the walls just do not hold up and I certainly blame the system and the Parole Board in most part for encouraging such methods of rehabilitation. Both Bette and her mother were told by the Parole Board, specifically, Chairman, Leonard McConnell, "that I would not have been paroled at all had it not been for the fact that we were married." I do not think that such an important step as marriage should be a requirement for parole.

We were married in the Trusty Division's visiting room by the prison chaplain. Not one of my more joyous occasions and neither was it an occasion that Bette was thrilled about either. But it worked and a few months later I received a parole. One other factor involved in getting that parole had to include, "admitting your guilt." Prior to receiving my parole I had seen the Parole Board on seven different occasions. Through my regular parole hearing dates and through two special parole consideration requests from officials here I was always denied a parole. The first man to put me up for a special parole consideration was Dr. Maurice Keyser. Keyser was the Chief Psychologist for the prison at the time, and although we didn't hit it off too well at first, I came to greatly respect his ideas and opinions.

Each time I went before the Parole Board I professed my innocence. That would only upset them and I would be sent away with nothing but a lecture on accepting responsibility for my actions. It made no difference to them what I said, did or showed them. If I wasn't guilty I wouldn't be in prison. It's as simple as that. The great State of Michigan does not make mistakes. That, my friends is wrong. There really are men in prison that do not belong there for what they have been accused of. I've met them. Hell, I'm one of them. In just the category of "murder" alone there is presently a book in publication that accounts the stories of 17 innocent men from Michigan who have served anywhere from two to 34 years in prison for crimes they never committed. Their pleas of, "I am innocent", fell on deaf ears and so long as they maintained such a plea of innocence they were to be denied a parole and remain in prison. It's a fact. It's happened. Those men were eventually released through court actions, private investigations, DNA testing and admissions by the real killers. The Parole Board never let them go. I salute these men who had the courage to stubbornly stand fast to their convictions.

In my case, I could not see the benefit of such stubbornness for 20 to 30 more years, to try and prove a point that would probably never be believed by anybody anyway. I certainly could not afford either financially or emotionally the hiring of yet another attorney and I most certainly didn't want to rot any longer in prison away from my children, family and freedom. So, after repeatedly being denied a parole by the Parole Board, it was Maurice Keyser who said, "That if I ever intended to get out, I would have to admit the crime." Reluctantly, the next time I saw them I did just that. Words to the effect, "Yes, I did it. I'm sorry." Well, the mood in that room for the first time in years changed from hostility to one of almost cordial friendship the next time I was to see them, and coupled with everything else we accumulated, I was paroled. It was a joyful morning to be sure when Bette picked me up in front of the prison and we drove to Saginaw and the home we would live in together. It was a large modular, three bedroom mobile home that looked like a palace to me especially after the last ten plus years of living in an 8x10 cell.

Living with Bette at that time was a tall blonde gal that went by several names who insisted on living in an espionage fantasy. Bette met this person a while after she met me in prison and together they established a firm relationship together. She was a dominate force in Bette's life. She seemed to live in that nether world between fantasy and reality, and I'm afraid she caught Bette up in her illusions. Often, I felt she found it difficult to separate the two and with the psychological problems Bette was facing while I was in prison she fell easily under this persons spell. Both were intelligent women. Both were suffering the aftermaths of a recent divorce. I feel the Castle Island endeavor helped to stabilize their lives somewhat at that time but upon reflection think that things would have worked out much more positively and productively if I would have held up the finances for that project until I was released.

They became immersed in the business which was good. But, by my not being there physically I became a convenient part-time owner, partner and source of financing their endeavors. As I've mentioned before through my various business ventures in prison I was pulling down more money than I made outside as a free man. Unfortunately this new partner entrenched herself too firmly into our lives. Bette began to rely upon her too much and by the time I was released from prison I ran head long into a competitive situation with my wife and her new girl friend.

After 10 plus years in prison it was hard to adjust back into a civilian and free life. So much was new, so many things had changed. Although I wanted to dive into the business and build something of a new life I felt myself being sidelined and relegated to the housework. Suddenly my ideas were no longer important or meaningful. I resented this situation and struck back by drinking too much. This also became a part-time hobby that Bette and her girl friend also indulged themselves in much too frequently. As will happen under those circumstances bad feelings began to generate, arguments escalated and I felt myself being pushed out of their lives. I really wanted to get my life back together and had illusions that Bette and I would be perfect together.

We bought some land in Harrison, Michigan and moved the modular to it. I worked hard in the move, digging the foundation and helping to tear apart and reconstruct the house. With another friend and business associate we bought a home in Grand Rapids, also in an effort to expand the business to that city. Somehow I ended up getting left in Grand Rapids while Bette and her new best friend commuted back to Saginaw to supposedly run the business. I was still only a few months out of prison and was seeing less and less of my wife; her time being dominated by her paranoid spy friend and her various illnesses and the business. To fill my empty days in Grand Rapids I became involved in the campaign of State Representative Thomas Mathew. I helped in his campaign for reelection by passing out circulars from house to house. I also went looking for a job in order to obtain money of my own rather than having to go to Bette or the undercover CIA agent for any spending money that I might need. Even though I had pretty much supported them for the past two years I felt like a beggar in front of them once I was out of prison. I didn't appreciate the feeling, and it was a position that I was not used to being subjected to.

So, if they didn't want me in the business I would step aside and let them run it. I would make my contribution to this commune through resources of my own. I would try to make enough on my own to pull Bette away to where we would be able to make it on our own and where I would be able to spend more time alone with her. But, the fates would not allow it. After a successful interview with a local Dodge dealership I was hired on as a new car salesman. Returning home with the good news I found that Bette and her friend had moved the majority of my belongings to a motel room on the other side of town.

Being on parole and knowing what a stiff, by-the-book parole officer I had, I knew there was nothing I could do about the situation. So, I accepted it and went on my way. Bette filed for the divorce and ultimately our separation became official. I hope they are happy together.

Chapter 6

A New Life

So, after the Betty and undercover agent separation I stayed in the Grand Rapids area and pursued my job at the Dodge dealership. Within a month I was the top salesman and on my way with a new life. I purchased some top of the line furniture for my new digs, a designer Lincoln Mark IV, and several three piece suits. I became more involved with the campaign of State Representative Thomas Mathew and at a Las Vegas night hooked up with a very outgoing young lady who also was working for the Representative. We hit it off immediately and became the best of friends. We dated often and life was good again.

I still had to report often to my Parole Officer who it was obvious was not a fan of mine so I had to watch my p's and q's. Driving up to his office in my new Mark IV in a three piece suit and reporting an income triple to his was just not something that an ex-con should be entitled to. He was jealous and let it show.

I soon became friends with my new friend's social circle and partied with them often. My income was such that I suggested that we start up an all girls bowling team and that I would finance it. So, once a week we were all at the lanes taking on all challengers. Suffice to say we were not going to threaten any world records or title holders. We were there to have fun and we did. I would often put up cash bonuses for strikes and scores and buy the rounds of drinks for the evening.

Then all hell broke loose. On one particular evening after a long deserved win I hung around with the girls and we drank the bar to closing. On my way home I desperately had to answer the call of nature so pulled off the main drag onto a side street and found a large tree in a residential neighborhood. I jumped out of the car and began to relieve myself. I swear I couldn't have been there more than a couple of minutes when two sheriff patrol cars pulled up abruptly and ran towards me and told me to get on the ground face down. They immediately put handcuffs on me and got me to my feet as I tried to explain to them what I was doing. But, to no avail, and they wrote me up for indecent exposure. This must have been a slow night for the sheriff's department. At any rate, when I was to eventually stand before the Judge he at least saw the humor in the situation as would any male who has at one time or other been in the same situation. The Judges comment was, "My goodness, this rates right up there with overtime parking. Get out of here. Case dismissed." Unfortunately my Parole Officer was also in the court room and requested that I report to him after I left court. I did, and he subsequently called upon the local police officials to report to his office, had me handcuffed once again and said he was going to violate my parole because he felt that I was now a danger to society. Ah, so much for someone trying to get ahead in life to a jealous parole official who couldn't.

After a couple of weeks spent in the County Jail, I was transferred back to Jackson Prison's Trusty Division. The Deputy Warden in charge of the Trusty Division was not a fan of mine because of past indiscretions at Jackson, and I'm sure with my Parole Officers blessings, made the obscured statement that he thought I was probably one of the most dangerous people in the State of Michigan and should be closely supervised. But, since my time/sentence would be up in less than two years there wasn't much he could do unless I violated the rules in some way. Thus, to make my time more memorable he assigned me to the pig farm and delegated me to cleaning out the pig stalls of their excrement on a daily basis. Fortunately for me, after a few weeks of getting cozy with the pigs the Deputy Warden had a mental breakdown, his second one I understand, and was sent to the local nut farm to recover. So another deputy warden was put in charge for which I did have a past relationship with which gave me the opportunity to request a transfer. It was granted and my next assignment was to the cattle farm where I herded cattle for the rest of my term. I actually enjoyed doing that as it got me outside in a sprawling pasture with lots of trees and pathways that I could walk around on all day. I was virtually under no supervision and lost myself in thought and nature. I did have the opportunity on a couple occasions to request a parole, but turned them down due to the fact I could max out my sentence in a few months. I did not see the advantage of being assigned to another overzealous Parole Officer and subjected to more supervision and scrutiny.

While I was in the farm system I found there was very little supervision and the inmate residents were able to score all forms of drugs as there were no fences, gates and tired guards, which made it easy to sneak out after lights out and run up to the county roads and pick up whatever package you had ordered that week. So, I bided my time; lifted weights, ran at least five miles every day and took it easy.

Finally my time was up and once again I was released and totally free with no parole hanging over my head and was picked up by my sister Judy who I lived with for the next several weeks. I secured another job selling cars with another dealership this time in Lansing and was once again on my way.

Shortly after my release when I came home from work one day my nephew was in the living room and wanted to introduce me to his babysitter, Michelle. He was sitting on the floor with her playing video games. She was without a doubt the cutest little thing I had seen in a very long time. At nineteen years old with big wide eyes and huge coke bottle glasses and a big wide smile. She was tall and slim and twenty-one years younger than I. "Hi" she said. "I've heard so much about you." Be careful Richard, I thought to myself, and proceeded to conduct myself as the perfect gentleman.

Well, one thing led to another over the next few weeks. Michelle would ride down from her house which was just down the block from my sisters on her horse to see me whenever she could, and then we would ride together across the fields of Mason. I found Michelle to be a fascinating young lady, full of unlimited energy, love, and excitement with a great outlook on life. We started to date off and on while I lived with my sister.

But now the time came when I had to move on. I had saved enough money to rent an apartment in town and did so. While Michelle and I were dating I soon learned that there were those who were a lot worse off than someone who spent time in prison. Michelle was brought up with a sister and two brothers to parents who owned and operated a dog kennel. It was her unfortunate lot to come home immediately after school and clean up to a hundred dirty dog cages each day. She would have to feed and water each dog and then proceed to clean the three bedroom house she lived in, after which she prepared dinner for the family and then washed the dishes prior to going to bed. Then it started all over again the next day. Her sister got out of that life as soon as she could and joined the Air Force. Her younger brothers were charged with other various duties around the house and property and suffered other indignities until they were old enough to escape their prison.

On one occasion in our relationship I offered to take her out to dinner. She reluctantly accepted. I say reluctantly, because she did not own a dress and had never been to a true restaurant other than a McDonalds or a Big Boy's. I wanted to show her a good time so bought her a dress and proceeded to take her to a very exclusive restaurant in Lansing. "Oh no" she said, "I can't go in there," panic beginning to rise in her. "And, why not'" I replied. "Because they won't let me" she answered. "Don't be silly" I answered. But the panic and fear was too great within her and we had to pass up this particular moment. It took me up to three tries before I convinced her it would be ok and that no one would throw her out. Even today I find it hard to believe that after nineteen years her entire wardrobe consisted of a pair of cutoff-levis and a single pair of jeans. The stories she has related to me over the years how her parents would make her and her sister and brothers wait in the car on hot summer days and cold winters while her parents went into town and spent hours shopping at stores for their needs only. Never had it seemed were there any purchases meant for them. Talk about a Cinderella life, this gal was living one. When she found out that I was going to move away from my sister she literally begged me to take her with me. Wow! Now what? Besides the kind of life I suspected she was living, there were hints that other things were taking place between her and her father which even today she is reluctant to discuss and I have never pressed her to that end.

Once, and prior to my moving out of Judy's I bought a bottle of wine and Michelle and I went into the country to park and talk and enjoy the stars and each other. We hadn't been there long when what should drive up but one of Ingham Counties finest. "Oh shit" I thought, here I go again. "May I see some identification sir?" I showed it to him and his eyes kind of squinted at me and then he asked Michelle to step out of the car. "How old are you miss?" he asked. "19" she said. "Is this man hurting you or holding you against your will?" Oh shit I thought again, here I go – another 30 years. "No sir, we're just good friends." Wheeew! I wheezed to myself silently. "Well, you can't park here. Move it along." My heart didn't stop pounding for the next hour.

So, now how was I going to answer Michelle about the apartment? "Look sweetheart, this won't work out. I'm way older than you are, and I'm sure as hell not ready to settle down." On and on I went about the many reasons this relationship wouldn't work. She wouldn't take no for an answer, so against my better judgment I consented to let her stay and try things out after I set some pretty stringent ground rules, all in my favor. She agreed, and quite frankly I didn't relish sending her back to that hell hole she was living in.

The apartment I rented was quite small and the furniture I brought from my Grand Rapids digs were rather large yet it never ceased to amaze me just how many different arrangements Michelle could get out of that stuff in such a small apartment. I swear that in the short time we lived there every time I came home it was a different scene. But no matter how late I came home, or how often, or even if I came home the apartment was always spotless. There was always a dinner ready and never a complaint. Well hell, maybe this arrangement can work out after all.

If I could ever consider myself good at anything, it was sales. I worked at a Volkswagen, Mazda and Volvo store in Lansing, Michigan in a General Motors town. Back then if you owned anything but an American car you were a traitor to the Country and the scorn of the automobile world. Yet I managed to average no less than 32 or more car sales every month over the next two years. I could do no wrong and got away with just about anything I wanted to at that dealership so long as I continued to produce. I came in late, called in with a hangover, came in drunk, took three hour lunches, and still never fell below 32 plus units a month. In fact it seemed the bigger the hangover, the more cars I sold. I also became very good friends with two other salesmen and we became pretty much inseparable over those years. They were also very good at what they did and between the three of us the dealership could always depend on no less than a hundred plus cars a month. Several times I can remember the owner in his office with is head in his hands on a late night when the three of us would stagger back from Happy Hour at the Playboy Club a few hours late and hardly able to walk, and just shaking his head and wondering, "Why?" But he never said a word when we handed him another one or two sales apiece before we left for the night.

Then there came the time when I received a call from an auto dealer in Florida, courtesy of my sister, Carol. She had told him of my abilities in car sales and he wanted to know if I might like to come to Florida on his dime and take a look around and maybe join his sales staff. Sure, why not. This was February in Michigan and cold as hell and an all expense paid trip to the sunshine state for the weekend sounded pretty good to me. I did ask if he wouldn't mind springing for another ticket for my unmarried salesman friend. He agreed and together we flew to Orlando where we were met by a chauffer and driven to Ft. Pierce. It was late Friday when we got there so we were handed the keys to the car and asked to report to the dealership on Monday. Our rooms should be ready at the Holiday Inn on the beach, and please feel free to charge everything to the dealership. Damn, what did my sister tell him about me? At any rate we played it to the hilt and had a great time lounging around the beach and pool for the weekend. On Monday we met with his General Manager who showed us around the place which quite frankly was quite small and not very impressive for a Cadillac/Pontiac dealership. He did explain that they were in the process of building a new dealership on the other end of town and should be ready in a year or so. No problem, but in the interim we did do a little investigation on our own when we had the chance to talk to his service manager and several other employees as to what type of an owner and person he was. Everyone including his General Manager trashed him to the max. Not good. So we thanked everyone and told them we would get back to them once we had a chance to digest and think it over and evaluate the move. Hell, there really wasn't a whole lot of thinking to do. We had a great time, and after about a month I called down to Florida and said thanks but no thanks. His General Manager called back a few days later and said he thought that would be our decision and informed us that he was about to quit and that he would be taking over another dealership in town that he so conveniently pointed out to us in his tour of Ft. Pierce. A much nicer dealership and it was. Well, that offer did spike an interest in me and after some serious thought; I called back and said, "Yes, I'll take the job."

A few months later, Michelle and I were on our way to sunny Florida after it was established that Michelle didn't have a problem with anything and all the rules remained the same. My sister Carol graciously gave us the use of her large fifth-wheel RV to live in until we found a more permanent place to stay. Barry Reed Buick, GMC, and Nissan was a crazy place to work. The owner, Barry Reed was a character like no other and should have a book of his own to publish one day. We got along and I sold him a lot of cars over the next six months. Apparently Barry liked me also and although he didn't want to lose me said that there was an opportunity opening up down the street that I might be interested in. Isuzu of America was coming into the country and opening a dealership down the street and was looking for someone to sell and promote their vehicles. "I think this would be really good for you Richard," he said. Well, bless his heart, it was.

A little scary I must admit, for when I first walked on the lot, it was apparent it was an old former gas station that had been closed for awhile with two very old used cars and two new "pup's" – Isuzu pickups- sitting on the lot. This was an opportunity? It sure as hell would be a challenge alright. But the guy I would be working for was very charismatic and I liked him immediately. He said he would really appreciate my help to get this place off the ground. I can't ever say I didn't like a good challenge and this sure as hell would be one, so why not? My new employer started buying used cars and Isuzu started shipping trucks. With a sales force of one we soon became a force of two then three and eventually six. Our little upstart dealership started to get recognized around town and within a year we were outselling just about every dealership in town. But, before I get ahead of myself, let me bring you back up to date.

The money was starting to roll in again and one day as Michelle and I sat across from each other we began to discuss where our relationship was headed. We had been living together now for over three years. We had obviously moved out of the fifth-wheel and I purchased a home in Pt. St. Lucie. We exchanged her coke-bottle glasses with contacts and performed some other cosmetic surgery that she needed very badly and as far as I was concerned she was still a living doll in my eyes. So, why not I thought. "Honey, ya wanna get married?" The answer was yes. So down to the court house for the license, and since neither of us were particularly enthralled with our Catholic upbringing opted out for the Justice of the Peace. We had the option of saying our vows in the court house or outside under the Gazebo in the garden. Definitely not the court room I thought to myself, as nothing positive could possibly come out of a courtroom. Little did I know at the time that the Gazebo was in a small courtyard situated between the court house and the county jail. Unfortunately the windows to the county jail were open so as the Justice of the Peace read the vows we were showered with wonderful shouts of, "Atta Boy Dude," "Give her one for me," and other such wonderful expressions flowing from the inmate population that we won't elaborate on at this time. I'm sure you can guess if you let your imagination run wild. But, on December 7, 1984 we made it through it and were now officially man and wife and still are today. After more than thirty years together and two lovely daughters, I am proud to say we are as much in love with each other as the day we said "I DO." So much for radio talk show host, Dr. Laura's opinion that May / December marriages don't work.

Once we started filling up the dealership with cars it was obvious I needed the best sales people available to move a vehicle whose name no one could even pronounce. So where better to go than back to Michigan and the two guys I knew could sell ice cubes in Alaska and my two best buds. I offered to move them both down lot stock and barrel. My single friend was the first to come. I loaned him a big moving truck and helped to get him a place to stay. A few weeks later I sent a truck up to fetch my other best friend and his family and possessions. I was able to find a home for his family and he was soon to arrive. We were together again and off on a new adventure that would eventually bring both joy and sorrow.

Ft. Pierce is a small older established town that sits on the eastern coast of southern Florida and the Atlantic Ocean with an accessible inlet that was/is a convenient drop for drug dealers. At one time, every boat or airplane that was suspected of carrying drugs into the mainland was reported on by the news media and they would broadcast pictures of the offending delivery and show the Coast Guard tracking the boat or plane on television. You could then watch as the various packages were being tossed overboard or out of the plane into the ocean. The ocean current would then invariably flow and distribute the suspected packages along the Ft. Pierce and St. Lucie inlets and onto the beaches. Well when those news reports were broadcasted across the airwaves, needless to say the next day at dawn, there would be an exceptional amount of joggers on the beach. Invariably you would be able to see and run out into the surf and quickly pick up a bail of marijuana or a tube containing several kilos of cocaine or heroin and then dash back to where your car was parked and throw the package in the trunk. There were just not enough Sheriff Deputies or State Police to patrol the vast sections of beaches along the coast. Plus it took them a long time to figure out what was going on. When they did, they of course stopped broadcasting the tracking of boats and planes over the various media outlets. That didn't stop anyone though as they just began to jog more frequently which became a favorite routine for many residents in the early morning hours.

I bring this activity up because on several occasions the enterprising salesmen in my employ would happen upon such opportunities and it soon became a growing problem within the dealership. Because of my recent background I wasn't about to snitch them out and I wasn't particularly averse to being a recipient of many large gifts from certain salespeople that had come across such treasures from the sea. I might also add that everyone that I hired in the dealership with the exception of my Office Manager were ex-cons. Best decision I ever made. They were all exceptionally hard working guys who received the respect they wanted and needed and made more money than they thought ever possible.

At that time a bail of marijuana was really the size of a bail of hay. A container of cocaine contained approximately three kilos of uncut cocaine. Another good friend and salesman of mine, who shall remain nameless, spent many a late night in a back office of the dealership cutting up kilo after kilo that washed ashore. We would then bag them into neat little 8-ball packages which he would then sell to prospective customers over the next several months. Fortunately we were never discovered or suspected of such dealings in all the time I was there, although it was beginning to get a bit out of hand shortly before the owner of the dealership sold everything to some rich Bahamian who thought he could sell cars.

The guys were starting to get sloppy and taking too many trips to the restroom during working hours. On a couple of occasions I would go into the bathroom after a salesman was in there and discover a line still drawn out that hadn't been snorted yet. That's all I needed was for a customer or who knows who to walk in there and see that. Obviously it was about time for me to end that little joyous activity and quick. We had a little meeting and the use of drugs at the dealership was no longer tolerated and I do believe that all respected that decision.

But the gang was somehow able to maintain and still sell cars and trucks. In fact in such great numbers that within a year we were number three in the nation in volume. The following year we became the number one dealer of Isuzu's in the nation. I now had the top three salesmen in the nation working for me and in 1986 I was subsequently named the top sales manager in the nation. Not too shabby when you consider that only three years prior we opened a car lot at an abandoned gas station on US-1 in the small town of Ft. Pierce. For three years in a row I was able shut down the dealership for five days and Isuzu flew us all to Las Vegas and put us up at either Caesar's Palace or the MGM. With all expenses paid we were treated like celebrities and sent home with even more thousands of dollars in our pockets. It was a great time to be in the automobile and truck business to say the least. But all that glory did not come without a lot of hard work and every single employee gave everything they had. I guess I did learn something from that crazy CO in the Marine Corps. If you all work hard together you get to play hard together. And we certainly did that.

Every weekend we would have an off-site sale somewhere in the city or county. We would have car wars with another dealer in the area. Once a year we would participate in a "Hand-A-Thon" with one of our sister stores, the Toyota dealer. To this date I've never seen a more successful or lucrative sales event in the automotive industry. This event grew by leaps and bounds every year. It was like looking down on the New York Stock Exchange. There were literally thousands of customers that came every year to purchase their cars and trucks on those days. We eventually had to move from the car lot to the Civic Center to accommodate all those that attended. It was a 24 hour event that only ended when the last person with his or her hand on the car was left standing. The sale generally lasted for 93 to 96 hours. In that time frame we would retail, deliver and finance over five hundred vehicles. The lowest commission check ever handed out to a salesman after the sale was usually over $5,000. The average check per salesman was between $15,000 and $20,000. Not bad for a couple of days work. We had salespeople from other dealerships take their vacation time during our sale just so they could work for us during "The Hand-A-Thons." We had wholesalers constantly bringing us vehicles to re-stock our used car inventory. Isuzu would divert auto carriers from the docks in Jacksonville straight to our sale. We were constantly moving vehicles in and out of the auditorium to make room for new ones. I had dealers calling me from around the country trying to figure out how to do what we were doing. Obviously, this type of a promotion took several months of planning, but always paid off in the end. For the five plus years we spent at Isuzu of Ft. Pierce we all had money coming out our ears. Every salesman that worked for me was knocking down six figures a year. We were a great family together. From the lot porter to the service personnel to the parts department to the sales guys and the office people, we were family, and my turnover was non-existent. We played and partied together and when possible even vacationed together. Even my head lot porter had his own demo and brought home over $80,000 a year.

Of course all good things seem to come to an end. Our owner had a group of twelve dealerships. Eleven of them were Toyota stores and belonged to the Moran group. It bugged them to no end that their one off-shoot, an – Isuzu – store was constantly outselling them and they couldn't figure out why. Hell, they still couldn't even pronounce the name correctly. So while we were on top of the heap so to speak, it for some reason seemed like a good time for him to sell.

As I stated earlier we were sold to some Bahamian millionaire for I'm sure multi-millions who owned Hutchinson Island off the coast of Pt. St. Lucie who then purchased several acres of land a mile down the road and assumed he could become an auto magnate. He put all his relatives in charge from the General Manager to sales and service managers. Within a year he drove that little Isuzu dealership right into the dirt.

There ought to be a law.

Fortunately we didn't have to hang around and watch the demise. Unfortunately I couldn't take my entire staff with me to the next store and I did have to watch the demise of some of my salesmen and friends. My Best Man, with an offer he couldn't refuse ran off to the other coast to become an RV salesman. A few others couldn't cut the white powder loose and lost their families and ability to sell anything. Those that stayed with me I took to an Oldsmobile dealership a few miles down the road and was installed as the Used Car Manager for Perona Oldsmobile.

While I was at Isuzu I had an advertising budget in excess of thirty thousand dollars a month. So, I pretty much owned the newspapers in the area when it came to advertising. I brought them with me to Perona's and we began to start all over again. Full color front and back pages of all the many publications in the area. We dominated the car ads. It was a Memorial Day weekend coming up and I learned that my prior owner at Toyota was planning a huge sale in the K-Mart parking lot across the street. So like any good football coach that gets traded I began my new plan of attack. I lined the front row of the dealership with all American made cars and painted all the windows with, "Made in America" Made by Americans" and "Buy American." Every antenna had an American flag attached to it; each entrance to the lot had an American flag. Each entrance also had huge column speakers that blared out John Phillip Sousa marches. My used imports were placed in a separate area with consentina wire surrounding them and I subsequently gave them the designation of POW's for quick sales. I had the newspapers photograph some of our local veterans planting an American flag through the roof of a Toyota that we painted the rising sun on both sides which was donated to us by the local salvage yard to represent the raising of the flag at Iwo Jima.

My full page color ads in all the papers showed one of my bald headed salesmen standing in front of the American flag reminiscent of the opening movie scene of "Patton". Below him was written, "On this date in 1943, Admiral "Toyota" launched a squadron of "Mitsubishi" planes from the decks of "Isuzu" powered aircraft carriers to destroy our brave men in the Marianas Islands. In honor of these brave men, Perona Oldsmobile will be closed this holiday. (Hell, I already made plans for the beach). But drive through the lot and if you see a vehicle you like and cut out this $500.00 coupon and bring it in Monday to apply to your purchase". On Monday we delivered thirty-two cars. Toyota across the street sold one, and closed down two days early.

Tom Perona, prior to our sale was deluged by phone calls from all the import dealers in town to pull the ad I created. All the domestic dealers on the other hand were delighted and got into the swing of things and all their vehicles sported American flags and window paintings and they in turn also had good Memorial Day sales. A credit to our owner who stood his ground and backed me up and told them, "I had to deal with him when he was with Isuzu. Now I've got him and it's my turn." In the short period of time that I was with Perona, we broke all used car sales records and were recognized by NADA (National Automobile Dealers Association) for doing so. Unfortunately, behind the scenes and unbeknown to me, Perona went out of trust with GMAC and had to close his doors. What a shame, but at least before we closed, our sales records afforded Michelle and I along with our sales staff and their spouses to be treated to a luxurious cruise aboard the Carnival Cruise Line to a few days in the Bahamas.

So now what and where to I thought. About a mile down the street was Buddy's Holiday Truck and Van. Buddy was an unusual character to say the least. He was a tall thin man who liked to drink and he partied hearty. But when it was time to work he was all business. Buddy had heard what happened at Perona's and asked if I would come up the street and see if we could get a jump start on his business which was selling RV's and a new used car lot that he had just opened. Buddy I might also add converted vans into luxury touring vans and they were the best built and produced vans on the market. But he was a smaller operation so once again I wouldn't be able to bring all my guys with me. I did bring along one of my top salesmen and my lot porter and once again we were in business. Like I said, Buddy was a hard working and aggressive individual who was a perfectionist when it came to building his creative vans and reconditioning other vehicles for his customers. But as I also said he liked to drink and not alone. So at five o'clock it was quitting time and at quitting time everyone had to stop what they were doing and meet in the garage where the bar was open and all were expected to partake in the merriment. It didn't matter if my salesmen were busy or if I was in the process of closing a deal. If we were not present in the garage he would come looking for us and actually introduce himself to the customer and very politely say in Buddy's southern drawl, "I'm sorry sir, but we all are closed. If you would like to come back tomorra I'm sure we can finish this up for you. Thank you." Believe it or not we never lost a customer, and if for any reason the customer may have looked a little perturbed he was soon laughing and whooping it up with the rest of us in the garage with a beer in his hand. This was also the time when some of the bankers in town would stop by on their way home to partake of some of the beverages offered. The banking business in those days was far different than it is today. In our business you dealt directly with the President or Vice President of the bank and if he put his signature on a deal it was a done deal. Most bankers in town knew of Buddy's generosity when it came to stopping for a toddy on their way home after the five o'clock hour. And stop they did just like clock work. Buddy would have their favorite beverage available and of course after a few drinks a deal that we were working in the office that usually would not have been approved under normal circumstances would creep into the conversation. Lo and behold the paperwork would magically appear and before the banking exec left the building we would have an approval from the lightly inebriated President himself to present to the bank the next morning. Not to shabby from that crazy hillbilly that worked down the street. This practice continued for as long as I worked there and never ceased to amaze me.

For the short period of time that I worked for Buddy we put together a couple of very successful sales. One in particular was a "Ladies Day" sale that required all the male employees to leave the dealership for the day. We turned the entire lot over to our wives and girlfriends. In addition I hired a few gals that I guess you could call, "ringers." In other words they were familiar with the car business in that they were F&I (finance and insurance) professionals that worked for other dealerships or sales gals from other dealerships, and the acting GM actually owned her own used car dealership. We began our advertising campaign several weeks before the sale was to begin with a radio blitz by local female disc-jockeys. All of our print ads were done in pink. We erected two very large pink tents and smothered them with pink balloons. The lady DJ's did a great job by intimating what guy wouldn't want to take advantage of a salesman's wife or girlfriend who probably didn't know anything about selling a car or RV. Meanwhile all the salesmen were gathered around my Tiki Bar and pool listening to the radio ads that broadcasted every 15 minutes of this incredibly unique sale going on at Buddy's Holiday Truck and Van on US-1. As we guys sat around and drank and ate and swam and listened to the live remote we could soon tell by the excitement in the DJ's voice that something extraordinary was happening. After a couple of hours we couldn't stand it any longer and so we all piled into our cars and headed for the dealership to see what was going on. Within two blocks of the place we ran into a huge traffic jam. By the way, two blocks on US-1 are very long blocks. When we finally made it to the dealership we confirmed our happiest thoughts and that was that all these cars were trying to get into the dealership. So we all gave each other high fives and headed back to the bar and pool and increased our shots to doubles. The next morning we were to find out that we sold over thirty RV's and conversion vans and ten used cars. My little pregnant wife, Michelle, actually turned in the biggest gross of the day. On the day of Michelle's conversion van delivery I spoke with her customer and he said, "Why hell, how could I turn down a cute little pregnant lady?" The sale was a huge success.

Within a month of leaving Buddy we made our mark on Ft. Pierce by being named and ranked as one of the top ten fastest growing businesses in the nation by "INC, Magazine."

Thus, after several very enjoyable months with Buddy there came a time when a local surgeon in town came into the office complaining about the treatment he was receiving from a local dealership in servicing his conversion van. They were rude and didn't service it right. "What does a person have to do to get some respect anymore?" "Well," I answered, "I guess you could always open your own dealership." Three days later the doctor walked back into the office with a brown paper bag in his hand and laid it on my desk. "Will this be enough to start my own dealership?" He asked. In the brown paper bag was over fifty thousand dollars in cash. "That's certainly a start" I replied. He also sweetened the pot by presenting us with the titles to his Rolls Royce, a Cadillac and a 32 ft. motor home. "You can use these also if you need them," He added. We sure could. I always wanted a Rolls for a demo. We shook hands and set up a meeting. Hell, I wasn't about to look a gift horse in the mouth. So, regrettably I told Buddy of my new plans which he certainly understood and we parted ways.

The next few weeks were consumed by meetings with the Doc and lawyers and my new partner, the top salesperson that I had brought with me. The Doc wanted to remain a silent partner which was fine with us. We brought along our faithful porter and opened up a lot on the St. Lucie/Martin County line on US-1. We were in a prime location and spent a lot of time setting things up right. Buying vehicles, licensing, hiring sales people, putting our porter to work in his own detail shop, and all the other neat things one must do to start a new business. I hired a guy by the name of Lee Hall to be our sales manager. Lee was a sharp guy and was also the best man for actor Burt Reynolds in his marriage to Loni Anderson. Burt would often stop by the dealership to pick Lee up and also purchased a couple of cars from us including a beautiful light blue Pontiac Trans-Am for Loni. Both he and Loni autographed a couple of large pictures of themselves which we proudly hung at the entrance of the office wishing us luck on our grand opening. Lee's wife Elaine was also Burt's Executive Director for his TV series, "Striker."

Michelle, after her short profitable career in the RV business was soon off to the hospital to give birth to our first daughter, Jessica. It was a hard birth; do to numerous mistakes made by her doctor. He incorrectly diagnosed her with a premature delivery two months early. Rushing her off to the hospital she bravely endured thirty- two hours in delivery. The on duty surgeon said it was too early and stopped the birth. Her doctor said "No" when he got there as Jessica had already entered the birth canal. So now with two more hours of induced labor and every blood cell in Michelle's body broken buy her pushing, Jessica finally entered the world too small and fragile, and was rushed off to an incubator where she would spend the next several weeks growing into life.

Things were now going along just great until against my better judgment, my new partner figured we needed to hire his wife to be our comptroller/office manager. Well, we did need one so I agreed so long as it was understood it would be a temporary position. In the mean time the Doc would make weekly visits to the dealership to see the progress and drop off more sacks of money.

As I have alluded to earlier while working at Isuzu my crew liked to indulge in the par-taking of the white powder, and my partner was no exception. Although an excellent salesman he had no clue as to what it took to run a business and we soon began to have numerous arguments about how it should be run. His wife, also a heavy powder freak had her ideas that together they could run this dealership much better than it currently was. Actually I thought things were going pretty well being a new dealership in town and averaging between 20-30 used cars a month and growing. After about six months the arguing and bickering began to get on my nerves and against my better judgment and ten plus years in the car business I just blew up and said, "Look, if you think you can do a better job, then buy me out and it's yours." Besides, I was starting to picture an axe growing out of his head and figured it was time to break away anyway. He agreed and we settled on a number of cars and cash that I would settle for and I was soon to retire.

As I suspected, within a three month period there appeared an article in the local newspaper that he was being sued by the Attorney General and a customer for fraudulent activities. I had also long suspected that he and his wife were cooking the books, so at the time I thought I was making the right decision. I was enjoying life and certainly did not want to return to the cross bar hotel for who knows how long for those same fraudulent activities and end up eliminating a jerk. Seems as though he was taking on consignments and when he sold them, he pocketed the money without paying off the loans the customer had on them. So much, I thought, for his fantasy expertise of the automobile business and office manager and the nose candy. Thus, "The Champion Connection" as we so aptly named the place was soon to be no more. In retrospect I should have bought him out and trudged on, but I was getting tired and didn't need the grief.

Somewhere in this time period, about three years after Jessica's birth, Michelle became pregnant again and we were excited about the arrival of a new member into the family. After a few months Michelle had an ultra-scan to see first hand what we had conceived, and lo and behold it was another girl. Within the allotted nine month time period we were introduced to our new little girl who we named Katherine. This birth went much easier. Late at night as is usually the case, Michelle woke me up and said it was time to go to the hospital, so quickly getting myself and Jessica dressed we hopped into the car and off to the hospital where we were met by the nurses who took Michelle away and told Jessica and I to go wait in the waiting room. I bought Jessica and me a coke and went to sit down and neither one of us had finished half our coke yet when the nurse came in the room and informed us of our new healthy family addition. I could not believe how fast this birth came as compared to Jessica's birth. We were able to view her before Jessica and I went home to spend the rest of the night and before going back in the morning to pick up a tired Michelle and beautiful Katherine.

I dabbled in the auto wholesale business and attended several auto auctions to keep myself busy while watching my meager retirement funds dwindle away at an alarming rate. My elaborate and fast track life was suddenly coming to an end once again.

Fortunately I was approached by a young lady that used to be a key figure in the handling of my advertising over the years and she asked if I would be interested in taking on the job as Sales Manager for the local newspaper in Stuart, Florida. Well, why not? After all, the t-paper situation at the Herr home was approaching critical. So I said yes and now was in charge of six sales girls in an all female dominated work place from the publisher to the editor to layout and design, etc., and I might add, they were all ten's. It didn't take a genius to figure out that advertising sales and supervising an office full of women was entirely different than running a used car lot full of alcoholic and drugged salesmen. You just couldn't throw one up against the wall and threaten to straighten them out if they didn't pay attention. This was especially hard to do with the pregnant ones. I mean, if you raised your voice to them they started to cry. Plus it never ceased to amaze me that at any given time at least two of them were experiencing that time of the month. They couldn't sell today because of a fight with their husband or boyfriend. They didn't like the customer because the customer didn't like them. It was too hot. It was too cold. On and on it went and although in the short year I was there we did somehow manage to increase our advertising revenue. I was also able to devise a plan for collecting from our deadbeat accounts which proved successful and which also kept them on as paying accounts. But this was not for me and it was time to move on.

So, now what was I to do? Seems I've been saying that a lot lately. The newspaper was running an ad for the fire department and so I thought, "Why not." I was still in pretty good shape and decided to give it a try. I was hired and immediately went into training which was vigorous, rigorous and physical, but still nothing like the Marine Corps puts you through in boot camp. I was actually having fun. The Jensen Beach Fire Department was a small unit that answered to every call in their area. Be it a fire, an accident or any emergency that occurred. There were several forest fires that we virtually leaped into, and at times not sure if we could leap out of. But we somehow managed to conquer the emergency. It was here that I realized just how hot a fire can get, when we answered a call to a local Ace Hardware and lumber store, and poured water on that establishment for over eight straight hours. We finally put it out but there was nothing left of the building. Everything was melted. The only item that survived was some nuts and bolts and those were eventually bulldozed into a pile to be shipped off to the local dump. Like I said earlier we responded to all calls, including auto accidents which at times were pretty gruesome. Like the time a Sherriff's deputy who had his legs severed at the knees by a drunk driver that didn't see his emergency lights because the deputy had his trunk opened and blocking what vision he had of those lights and subsequently slammed into him. Or the time a guy threw his girlfriend out of his car traveling over sixty miles an hour, or the five teenagers celebrating prom night and slammed into a brick wall and killing three of them. Of course in Florida you have hurricanes. When I would get the call, always it seemed, in the middle of the night. Michelle would say, "Richard, you can't go out there on a night like this." I would always have to remind her that, that was my job and all would be fine. Often we would spend up to 36 hours in the truck going from one emergency to another. It's really incredible what the wind can do, especially when they also spawn tornadoes with vast amounts of destruction.

I really enjoyed the fire department and often wish I could have joined many years earlier. It's to say the least a very honorable profession, and one with brave men and women that run into danger instead of away from it, and give of their lives freely to save those of us in need. Following the Marine Corps, you guys have one of the hardest jobs out there. I salute you. But, there came a time once again when it seems in my nature to screw up. And so I did. Yup! It was now time to spend a little more time in the cross-bar hotel.

While I was working with the fire department I supplemented my income by painting and drawing, and one day I was working on the design of a tee-shirt for one of our local watering holes in Jensen Beach. Everyone was happy with my designs which I was creating at the bar with the patrons and bartender constantly plying me with beer and demon rum. It soon became apparent that I had better leave when my drawings became more and more Picasso-esk, and I would soon reach an unconscious state of mind. I foolishly crawled into my car and headed home and was just a block away when I slammed into an elderly couple's car. I didn't do too much damage to either car or the "blue hairs" as they are so often referred to here in Florida. Of course in my present state of mind I figured I'd better take off and get home before anyone noticed what I had just done.

Wrong move! A good citizen had seen what happened and followed me home. It wasn't long before a couple of Martin Counties finest were knocking at my door. "Is that your T-Bird out there sir?" "Ah, no. I think it could be my neighbors a couple of blocks over" I said. They didn't see the humor in my response and it was off to the hooscow in no short order. I think I spent a couple of weeks in there which after 12 years of doing time wasn't too bad. Fortunately, I had a few friends out there who came to my rescue, and being with the Fire Department helped. I was sentenced to a few weekends in jail. I served those and too embarrassed to go back to the fire department figured it was time to say goodbye to sunny Florida.

CHAPTER 7

Michelle and I rented a big 26ft. Penske truck and loaded up all our worldly possessions, Jessica and Katy and our faithful Great Dane, Tiger Lilly, and headed back to Michigan without a clue as to where we would end up or support ourselves. After a leisurely two and a half days of travel we ended up in the driveway of one of my daughters. She and her husband graciously agreed to put us up until I could find a job and a place to live. We all slept on her living room floor for about two weeks before I just happened to stop at a Pontiac Dealership and lo and behold, who do I run into but my long lost buddy, and his family who had also retreated back to Lansing. Of course he was their leading salesman and it didn't take much convincing of the management to hire me immediately.

Within the next few days we found a house to rent just down the block from my daughter and we were off on life's new adventure. I spent about a year and a half at this Pontiac dealership until I secured new employment at an Auto Mall across town as their new Mazda/Volvo Sales Manager. The year was 1995. Car sales at that time were slowing down in the State and we lost our Finance Manager, so I was now to assume the positions of both Sales Manager and Finance Manager of the Dealership. But despite the state wide sales slow down I still managed to pull both Mazda and Volvo from last place to the number one spot in their division. During this time I lost my Mother to cancer. A two plus pack a day smoker she went suddenly with no warning. It wasn't that long ago that I was playing golf with her in Florida. She loved the game and was also a score keeper for the LPGA. She was vibrant and always full of energy and was the last person anyone in the family would suspect of passing off before dad.

Pop had lost the use of his legs and mom was taking care of him which I know was a strain on her. Her passing was a severe blow to him and he just gave up and we had to place him in a convalescent home. Unfortunately I wasn't able to be with mom when she died as I was living in Lansing at the time and she went suddenly without warning. But my sister Judy and I flew down to Florida to be with her before her cremation which is what she and dad had decided on when it was time. But I did feel the need to be next to dad now in his time of need. So, regrettably I resigned from the Auto Mall and yes moved back to Florida. I took a job at the Interstate Auto Auction as General Sales Manager in Ocala where dad was staying. In his last days I believe we grew closer together than any time in our lives. I would check him out often from the home and take him four-wheeling in the sand dunes around my sister Carol's house, smoke cigars, and do double shots and whatever other sinful things I could think of to make his last days as enjoyable as possible. I even cruised the seamier strips in town with him to find a woman of ill-repute, but to no avail. I think he was having a good time and hope I didn't contribute to his final demise. But except for our times together he was not a happy camper. He really missed his wife of 50-plus years, his health was regressing rapidly and he hated the indignity of not being able to control his bowel movements. Then there came the inevitable phone call that he was taken to the hospital suffering from a massive stroke. I immediately went to him and could see that he was not going to make it. I stayed with him through the night and could only hold his hand and communicate with him through yes and no eye blinking as he was unable to talk. He did have a living will and had often said in our lucent times together that he did not wish to be a vegetable. He was presently on life support and the doctors wanted to know what they should do. I spent another few hours alone with him trying to communicate as to what his wishes would be. I called my sister Judy in Michigan of what the situation was but she didn't feel she could afford the trip. Carol was off at a dog show somewhere so I ultimately made the decision to have them pull the plug. I knew that is what he wanted and I would have felt the same if it was me. I will never forget the look in his eyes as I told him it was time. He was scared and unsure but also knew there was no other alternative. The doctors and nurses told me to go home and get some rest. The Auction house was just over a mile away so I did decide to go there to let them know I may be taking some time off when the call actually came as I was talking with my secretary. I rushed back to the hospital and dad was in a coma. Within the hour as I held his hand he joined his beloved wife. I remember my daughter, a registered nurse, telling me to talk to him, that even in a coma state he would be able to hear and understand me. I truly hope that was the case.

It was less than a month after dad died that we were notified at the Auction that the owners had decided to sell the 31 acres of land to an industrial development next to where we were located just off of I-75. So now what? Well goodbye Florida once again. I had always wanted to move out west as I had often passed through Nevada, New Mexico and Arizona on my way back and forth from California to Michigan. My sister Carol was not willing to sell us an acre of land off the ten acres she already owned so I did not see any alternative or advantage to stay there. So Michelle and I sold the house, packed up another 26ft Penske and hit the road west. We traveled slow and easy and spent every night in a Best Western on the way because they all had pools and the girls loved swimming before bed. We finally arrived in Flagstaff Arizona in April of 1998.

We spent the day getting our affairs in order. Opened a bank account and looked for a place to live. We found one and spent the rest of the day unpacking and unloading the truck. It was a nice sunny day at the base of Mount Elden. Imagine our surprise when we awoke the next morning to a foot of snow. Welcome to Flagstaff. After twelve years here and living on top of a mountain at seven thousand feet in the air we have learned that you can actually expect to see snow in the middle of summer. But it usually melts by mid afternoon. Overall, it's a beautiful city and place to live. You cannot stand anywhere in this city and turn in any direction at any time of the day and not be overwhelmed by its magnificent scenery and beauty. For many years it has been nominated as the city with the cleanest air in the country. But enough as a tour guide.

For the first two years in Flagstaff I pretty much just goofed around. I joined the local Chamber of Commerce, and traveled the historic confines of the city and sat at my favorite bar and with trusty pencils and pad I drew the sights and citizens as they passed by. I had three art shows around town and sold a few pictures and drawings which helped to support the family for awhile. But, as one soon learns here, the saying that Flagstaff is, "Poverty with a View" is a true statement. Things ain't cheap here. Thus, I had to find a job. Within a few days I was back in the car business as an assistant sales manager for the local Dodge dealer in town. It didn't take long to find out that the owner was a consummate greed machine. In addition to my duties in sales and closings and handling numerous complaints from customers I was also handling complaints from his employees. I don't think a week went by that I wasn't going to him or the office manager over a shortage in an employee's paycheck. This guy had a pay plan worked out that I don't think former U.S. Secretary Greenspan could even decipher. At any rate, the straw that broke the camels back was when he had me fire a lot porter because his son told him that he was drinking on the job. This poor porter had a speech impediment, had a new wife and an infant son and hitchhiked thirty miles every morning to and from work so he could take care of them. I investigated the charges thoroughly and found the charges to be false and related such to the owner. He didn't care and ordered me to drive him home. I did, but such cruel and inhumane acts became common and I no longer could justify working for such a person.

As Sales Manager, I would often wholesale vehicles to other dealers around town and had an occasion to meet a used car manager from another dealership that I enjoyed selling to and trusted. It only took a few sales to see that this guy probably was one if not the sharpest car guy in town. Via my years in the car business I pretty much knew what to look for and usually came out on top when it came to either the retail or wholesale of automobiles. This guy knew all of the tricks too and I admired him for that, so when it was time to say goodbye to the Dodge guys I called him and was working with him the next day. As I stated earlier this was an honest guy and we pretty much thought the same way as far as the automobile business and life in general goes and we soon became good friends. So, for the next few years we worked together and made a few dollars.

Then there came the time when he was approached by someone who wanted to open a new dealership in town and wanted him to manage it. Well, it just so happened that this someone was, the someone, I couldn't stand and left a few years earlier. My new partner of course wanted me to go with him and I just couldn't see myself doing that. Consequently, negotiations with the Dodge guy proceeded to the point where an offer was made that we in good conscience could not refuse. The Dodge guy actually kept his word and for the next several years things went fairly smooth. We opened a trailer and RV dealership along side the car dealership and happiness was within reach until the better of Mr. Greed showed his ugly face again. He thought he was smarter and better than the local County Board of Supervisors and of course it wasn't long before the Board proved him wrong and red tagged his business. Mr. Greed eventually lost everything. Chrysler pulled his franchise. Hyundai did the same and the trailers all went to who knows where.

It once again looked like retirement was once more in the stars for me. But, throughout my stay in Flagstaff I joined the local Marine Corps League and the Toys for Tots organization and became very active in both. I was to eventually become President of the Marine League Charities and for the next year was kept busy helping out with various charitable events raising money for the Toys 4 Tots, the Wounded Marines and local school FAAST programs. Every year for eight plus years I was to be Santa Clause for the Marines and various City events and still hope to stay Santa for as long as I am able. The one thing I've learned in that capacity is that we're all going to be alright. These kids I see in every economic and social level are smart, sharp, compassionate and indulgent. One of my proudest moments at this time was to receive the "Marine of The Year" memorial award in 2007.

Hence, I have now taken you through a life that has seen justice and injustice with a lot of hardship and some prosperity, love and hatred, sane moments and drugged induced moments. What have I learned and what have you learned throughout this journey and the purpose of this book? Well, I hope that you must see that it is imperative that you keep and maintain a certain sense of humor or life will be unbearable and not kind to you. Most of all, you must never judge a book by its cover. Never underestimate or overestimate anyone or anything in this life or you will get bit.

Finally, I'm sure there are still a lot of questions that you have that have not been answered to your satisfaction, in particular the murder of Mrs. Betty Reynolds. Believe me, I'm just as curious and ill informed as you, but will try to answer to the best of my ability. Such as, why would I or anyone plead guilty to something that they didn't do? Why haven't I pursued the alleged conspiracy against me by the Eaton County judicial system and my so-called legal defense? Why would I not, after twelve years in prison pursue the person or persons who in fact were the murderers of Betty Reynolds?

I believe I answered the first question at the beginning of the book. But, to reiterate; most people when arrested are incarcerated in a dormitory type cell. Meaning you are sequestered with several other inmates with access to a television set, books, a deck of cards, newspapers, a radio or various board games. But most important you are able to talk, and interact and socialize with other men. In solitary confinement you have no contact with other people other than your jailer who you seldom see or converse with, and when you do, it is to follow orders and you're looked upon as scum of the earth. He's the guy who is always searching you or shaking you down. There is no intelligent conversation with this person. You have absolutely no contact with the outside world. No news, no TV, no radio, no music, and you don't even know what the weather is like outside. You don't know if the wind is blowing, snowing or its raining. You're confined in a 4x8 foot space surrounded by three cement walls and a row of iron bars in the front. Your only sense of entertainment is in your own mind. The food is crap and monotonous. So day after day stretches into week after week and month after month – eight and a half of them to be exact – that's three quarters of a year and over 50 pounds lighter. Your only information is received from your attorney or 15 minutes a week from your wife assuming she is able to make the 20 to thirty mile trip.

Eventually you hunger for another voice or another person to react with. You will eventually agree to anything that's presented to you, right or wrong, just to feel like a human being again. I sold my soul for a pack of gum every other month. If I would have had an inkling of what was going on, what to look for, what to expect, I probably could have lasted a little longer. Knowing that I was going to say, Yes, to something that I didn't do held no bearing on anything other than to change my environment and knowing full well I was wrong to do so, and once I did it, it was too late and I was through. Of course knowing what I know now things would have been different.

Number two; why haven't I tried to sue or go after those who prosecuted me? Well let me in turn ask you this. For what purpose would that serve? Do you actually think any one of them would admit to any wrong doing? Think about it. How many times in your lifetime have you ever been privy to the State admitting that they were wrong? They are the political and judicial power and authority in a small urban county. They can do no wrong. Most involved are now dead, have left the State for places unknown or voted out of office. They have already been found guilty of abusing their power while in office, and I refer to Judge Robinson, the prosecutor, the Sheriff and the arresting officer. Squeaky clean saints they weren't. How much time and money would it have cost me to say, "I told you so?" Both money and time I did not have. I had already lost too many years. It was time to get what was left of my life back.

Finally, Why not at least get the s.o.b that framed me and put me there? I'll admit that's a hard one. I am still in somewhat of a conflict on that one and I have thought about it more often than I care to. I do feel I know what happened, but proving it at this late date would be next to impossible. The evidence and witnesses have all but disappeared. The principles have either died or fled the State. Would I now destroy the lives of two girls who may have believed what they thought was true? Or, would I be the one who is wrong? Even though all evidence and motive points in one direction, could there be another explanation? One theory that was bantered about was that Pauline, a jealous wife, followed me out to the Reynolds house and committed the deed. I have never believed that for a second, but, it's another possibility of perhaps many. God knows I've seen enough wrongly accused people in my time. And, once again, there is the time and money factor. My children have already expressed their aversion to dredging up this whole affair again after the ridicule they have had to endure throughout their lives, and to what purpose would that serve? Whoever was responsible will eventually receive their true punishment at the hands of the one true judge. What more could one ask for?

In the Marine Corps I saw mans inhumanity to man. I've seen poverty at its worse. I've witnessed the birth of my children, and traveled the country and world to a limited extent, and enough to see the beauty and devastation it can offer. I've seen the best in people and the worse in people. I've been able to provide for a family and watch my children grow into mothers and fathers and raise children of their own. With fifteen grandchildren and one great grandchild and still building I must consider myself somewhat redeemed and blessed. Granted, I've made some bad decisions and some good decisions and only time will tell and be able to distinguish which is which. I do not regret my life and at 69 years of age can still look forward to the many joys and new experiences that are still on the horizon. If this book has any value to anyone, it is to see and learn that life isn't over till it's over. Never give up, because a new life and experience is just waiting over the hill and I'll be damned if I'm going to miss it. The original title of this book was to be, "To Be Continued," but someone beat me to it. But the hell with that, I'm just getting started. – TO BE CONTINUED…

Author R Herr on the left with cohorts watching football
in the Spectator Office, also known as the location of
the best brewed "Spud Juice" within the joint. 1973

Paul "Harry" Amedeo DeRose, Father-in-law, businessman and gambler.

"The Dragons Den" mural painted by Author R Herr & Mac McBee,
better known as a sanctuary behind the walls of Jackson Prison

Author R. Herr far left with Black Mafia
members at Jackson Prison 1971

Left to right; Jackson Prison Warden Perry Johnson
being interviewed by Author R Herr
on Closed Circuit TV Show, "The Chair" 1968

Aerial view of the State Prison of Southern Michigan in
Jackson, MI; the largest walled prison in the world.

Inside of cell block: landing on the terrazzo floor 5 stories below usually silenced most snitches forever.

Looking down on the main yard at Jackson Prison. The large building in the center was 15 block. It was better known as "The Hole", where the so-called unruly resided. Long since torn down.

Inside Jackson Prison with flower garden on the left and
15 block, "The Hole" on the right. You did not want
to go there. Neither entities exist at this time.